THE
VERDICT
OF HISTORY

Other Books by Author

The Resurrection Debate
The Resurrection of Jesus: An Apologetic
The Resurrection of Jesus: A Rational Inquiry
Verdict on the Shroud

THE VERDICT OF HISTORY

CONCLUSIVE Evidence for the Life of Jesus

GARY R. HABERMAS

THOMAS NELSON PUBLISHERS
Nashville

ISBN 0-8407-5919-3

With Love to My Parents,
Robert and Roberta,
Who first told me about Jesus

Contents

Contents

Part Two: Historical Data Concerning Jesus' Life

Contents

Acknowledgements

I am grateful for the assistance of several persons who contributed to this present volume. William Lane of Western Kentucky University and Grant Osborne of Trinity Evangelical Divinity School both read the complete manuscript and presented helpful suggestions, especially concerning the bibliography. Edwin Yamauchi of the University of Miami of Ohio and Russell File, librarian of Liberty Baptist College, also provided bibliographical assistance. Thomas Nelson Publishers and editors Ronald Pitkin and Paul Franklyn, in particular, deserve special thanks for their work in so quickly, efficiently and smoothly expediting the editorial duties for this book. I would like to thank the fine secretarial help supplied by my own institution in typing the manuscript. As always, I also appreciate my wife Debbie and my family for tolerating my long hours of writing.

Introduction

As my fourth book on the topic of the resurrection of Jesus, this volume is an attempt to point out another aspect of the truly exceptional historical and scientific evidence for this event. The earlier books dealt, respectively, with the failure of naturalistic and other alternative attempts to explain away this occurrence, the possible scientific evidence from the Shroud of Turin and an apologetic which proceeds from the resurrection of Jesus to Christian theism as a whole. While this book is thus another puzzle-piece in the complete apologetic, it is a piece which can stand alone in producing a very important element in the total case for the resurrection of Jesus.

This book is chiefly an effort to examine the life, death and resurrection of Jesus from another and somewhat different perspective. It is largely concerned with pre- and non-biblical evidence for these events. In other words, the main body of this book is devoted to a study of sources which date from before, during and just after the New Testament itself. As such it presents both a fascinating and largely unknown subject. This book is divided into three sections. The initial portion deals with issues which must be covered before we can attempt to deal with the actual ancient sources for the life of Jesus. Chapter I is a brief statement of historical methodology, including a section on a historical response to miracle-claims. The next two chapters are concerned with attempts to dehistoricize a portion or all of Jesus' life, both more technical (Chapter II) and more popularistic (Chapter III) examples.

Part II presents the key thesis of this book—the pre- and extra-biblical evidence for Jesus' life. Consecutive chapters deal with non-Christian sources (IV), pre-New Testament creeds, including the facts which critical scholars accept as historical (V), non-New Testament, Christian sources (VI), and archaeological evidence (VII).

In this second section the source material is usually dated from 30-130 A.D., or within approximately 100 years after the death of Jesus. However, there are several sources that extend up about 150 years after this event. An effort has been made to include virtually all of the sources during these years, but by no means is it claimed that this is an exhaustive treatment.

The last chapter summarizes the facts of Jesus' life and concludes with a synopsis of the evidence of his death and resurrection, in particular. The final material includes both an appendix in outline form that summarizes the various critiques of those who attempt to "debunk" Jesus' life and another appendix which provides a technical bibliography of the Gentile sources.

An Important Concern

An important question is often raised as to why we should be so concerned with pre- and extra-biblical material when we have plenty of information about Jesus in the New Testament. There are both positive points to be raised and warnings to be given with regard to such a methodology.

Positively, there are a couple of related reasons for exploring sources for Jesus' life which are found outside of the New Testament. Initially, such an effort has much apologetic value because of the possibility that this data might corroborate our present knowledge on this subject. In other words, we may find additional evidence for the events of Jesus' life, death and resurrection which strengthens the case derived from the Scripture. Additionally, this entire topic is one on which comparatively little published research has been done. Therefore, since at least some important evidence is to be gleaned from these sources, it ought not be largely ignored by Christian scholarship.

On the other hand, there are some implicit dangers which we cannot ignore. Therefore, a warning must be issued along with the plea that readers not take this concern lightly. Namely, by pursuing this line of pre- and extra-biblical evidence we run the risk of implying that Scripture is not a sufficient source of knowledge about Jesus or that we need additional information about his life. As a consequence, one might ignore Scripture as the primary witness to Jesus or doctrine might be questioned unless extra-biblical evidence could be adduced.[1] By such explicit or implicit beliefs, much of New Testament theology would be ignored or compromised.

This writer does not wish to be a part of such efforts that teach or even imply that Scripture is not a sufficient basis for Christian belief. This book is devoted to developing a new area of apologetics and not to questioning the basis of Scripture in any way.[2] In fact, this writer believes that the best approach to apologetics (in general) is one which begins with the evidence for the trustworthiness of Scripture and which then proceeds on this basis. Thus, the approach of this book should not be viewed as the author's normative apologetic approach.

Notes

[1]See Chapter II,C for a refutation of such views.

[2]It should be remembered that this book fits into a complimentary whole with three other books by this writer on the subject. One of those books (see Gary R. Habermas, *The Resurrection of Jesus*. Grand Rapids: Baker Book House, 1980. Appendix 2), which argues from Jesus' resurrection to Christian theism as a whole, presents a detailed defense of the inspiration and inerrancy of the Scripture. This doctrine is based on the testimony of Jesus and vindicated by his resurrection from the dead. That section also contains a specific treatment and rejection of approaches which misuse or ignore this basis in Scripture.

PART ONE

Contemporary Approaches to the Historicity of Jesus

1

Historical Methodology
and Miracle-Claims

In this chapter we will look first at the concept of history that will be used in this book and then view the method of historical investigation. Later we will turn to the relationship between historical investigation and miracle-claims.

A. A concept of history

The term "history" is used in various ways by different scholars. There is no uniform definition which is agreed upon by all historians, as numerous approaches and interpretations are commonly utilized.[1] Therefore, it is not our purpose here to present a treatment of the contemporary definitions of history. However, it seems that there is at least some general agreement concerning the content of history.

Historians are virtually agreed that history includes at least two major factors—the actual events in particular and also the recording of these events. Thus this discipline is mainly concerned with what has happened and how these occurrences have been annotated and interpreted. It is this conception which will form the core understanding of history as it will be used in this book. Other elements are surely involved, as will now be noted. But the inclusion of these two major ideas are essential and are thus the foundation of this concept.

Now we surely do not mean to affirm that the presence of these two elements is all that is involved in a definition of history. Rather, these are the ones which seem to recur most often. However, a few other factors that are part of this discussion should also be mentioned briefly.

First, there is always a subjective factor involved in the writing of history. For instance, the historian must select the material which he will (and will not) cover. The historical event itself is objective. It is the recording and interpretation of the event that introduces subjective factors. For W. H. Walsh, the subjectivity of the writer is present, but it is not a really serious roadblock to obtaining objective history. This subjectivity can be allowed for and its efforts can be overcome.[2] The best approach to take toward history is one of caution, as we should try and recognize this subjective bias and then make the proper allowance for it.[3]

An excellent example of dealing with this subjective factor occurs in the study of ancient history. The works of Tacitus provide a case in point. This Roman historian is known to have had prejudices, such as his "aristocratic bias" and his conviction that moralizing was the "highest function" of writing history. Sometimes inaccuracies cloud his text, such as attributing speeches to persons who never gave them or incorrectly reporting details in battle accounts.[4] As one historian asserts, the interpretations of Tacitus "must often be challenged" because he "could see only through his own lenses which were strongly colored."[5]

Does this mean that we do not accept Tacitus as a viable source for ancient history? Do these subjective elements in his writings invalidate the historical information which he imparts to his readers? Strangely enough, Moses Hadas states that Tacitus was Rome's greatest historian:[6]

> One may well ask how trustworthy the resultant history is. A modern historian guilty of such faults would surely lose all credit.... With allowance made for rhetorical embellishment customary in his day, and within the limits of distortion which his own views of morality and politics make inevitable, Tacitus never consciously sacrifices historical truth.[7]

Michael Grant shows how the example of Tacitus is not isolated in ancient history. Herodotus mixed legends and anecdotal material in his histories, while Livy made room for the interplay of omens. Even worse, both Livy and Tacitus are examples of ancient historians who wrote about events which occurred much earlier, sometimes up to as much as five centuries before. One result is that there are frequently inconsistencies and contradictions in these ancient writings.[8]

But historians do not despair of reconstructing the ancient past. As we saw with Tacitus above, these scholars make allowance for the subjective recording and interpretation of the events, as well as for incorrect data, and still arrive at the valid facts of the past. Ancient history relies on these abilities.[9]

We will also endeavor to allow for this subjective factor in our investigation of the life, death and resurrection of Jesus. Although we are dealing with first century A.D. Palestine, we have seen that historical investigation is still capable of ascertaining objective data concerning the facts which did occur.

Second, we find that history cannot reach the point where it is totally positive of its findings in all instances. As with physics, so there is also a certain amount of dependence on probability in history as well.[10] For instance, Ernest Nagel admits that he accepts a deterministic view of history in spite of the convictions of contemporary physicists who almost unanimously hold the opposite viewpoint. The conclusions of these scientists have had an affect on historians, for the accepted scientific view against a deterministic universe has also helped to turn historians against a deterministic view of history.[11]

Nagel lists five main reasons why historical determinism is generally rejected by so many historians today. First is the argument from the absence of any developmental laws or patterns in history. This discipline does not follow according to laws or precepts which would determine certain outcomes or occurrences in advance. Second is the argument based on the inability to explain and predict events in human history. In spite of frequently repeated ideas to the contrary, history cannot be predicted when based upon past events or other such data. The future is not based on the past in this sense. The third argument concerns the appearance of the novel in historical occurrences. New events and the configurations of new ideas recur throughout history. Fourth is the argument from those chance events which are also a part of history. Frequently, "strange" events occur in history which were unexpected and even out of the ordinary. The fifth argument concerns the conflicting results when one attempts to make the concept of a deterministic world compatible with the freedom and moral duty of human beings. Such freedom entails a creative aspect in history based upon human choice. As instances of the above five points, who could have predicted the spread of a novel culture from a war-like community in third century B.C. Macedonia? Or who could have anticipated that an entire civilization would grow from a seemingly barbaric people on the banks of the Tiber and finally emerge in the first century B.C.? It is because of these and other similar findings that so many historians have rejected the deterministic view of history. Nagel states further that the findings of modern physics, which also oppose determinism, have been a key factor that has exercised a direct influence on a similar rejection of this concept by most historians.[12]

The appearance of these chance and novel events mentioned above, together with the aforementioned inability to explain or predict many other occurrences, has helped to further the use of probabilities in historical studies (as well as in scientific investigation). Historians recognize and utilize this concept of probability.

Wand notes that we cannot be as sure of historical investigation as was thought possible in the past. However, we must make our judgments as to which facts are most probable according to the historical evidence.[13] For this reason Montgomery opts for a critical investigation of the sources in question, with the decision about the occurrence of any specific event being based upon the probability of the evidence. In fact, probability is referred to as the only sufficient guide for a historian.[14]

It must be carefully noted here that the use of probability does not preclude certainty in matters of well-established historical events. Such events which are validated by careful historical research (and especially those which have been established for long periods of time) are proven facts. If further data is found which casts doubt on such an event, it might be necessary to reopen the investigation. But precluding any such contrary material, the fact may be viewed as certain, or as proof. For example, there is no good historical reason to doubt the death of Julius Caesar by assasination, Napoleon's defeat at Waterloo or the election of Abraham Lincoln as the sixteenth president of the United States. These facts are sure at this time and thus proven to be certain.

These elements, then, are to be included in a contemporary treatment of history. While it has not been our purpose to deal with this subject in depth,[15] we will refer to history as both the occurrence of past events and the recording and interpretation of them. Realizing that there is always a certain amount of the subjective in this recording, allowance must be made for it as much as is possible in order for objective data to be obtained. Realizing also that in speaking of history we are dealing with probabilities, it will be our desire to ascertain as nearly as is possible which facts best fit the evidence. With these probabilities and uncertainties any event is possible. Events cannot therefore be ruled out (either scientifically or historically) before they are researched. The only answer is a thorough investigation of the evidence. Events which are firmly established by historical investigation may be viewed as certain, proven facts.

B. Historical research and investigation

For historians the occurrence of past events can be discovered (within a certain probability) by a careful investigation of the facts. Since these events happened in the past, they are only accessible by a study of the historical evidence. Although the historian himself will not be able to participate in the event that has already occurred (unless he was originally there), he is able to inspect the relevant data such as the eyewitnesses, written documents and various other records, structures or archaeological finds. Upon such confirmation the historian must obtain his evidence. This is the working principle of historical research.[16]

Of course, what the existing data and written sources reveal is not usually automatically accepted as true. It is therefore the job of the historian to critically investigate the available claims in order to ascertain as closely as possible what has happened. This includes the procedure of determining if the sources best support the claims that are made in them. The proper results can be obtained even though there exists this need to determine which facts best fit the evidence. Then it is the duty of the historian to formulate the facts based upon this groundwork.[17] One is to decide upon the evidence at hand—that which is shown to be the most probable conclusion.

To investigate the past in such a manner, there must be historical sources for the data. These are usually divided into primary and secondary sources, with the former being much more critical for the historian. Primary documents include both literary and non-literary remains. Primary literary remains include written documents which may be official or unofficial. The former would usually be composed by an official or representative of the state, such as Pliny the Younger's famous correspondence, written while he was a Roman governor in Asia Minor during the first century A.D. The latter would include informal works such as books, newspapers, journals or periodicals, such as Julius Caesar's accounts of his battles in Gaul, written before his rule in first century B.C. Rome. The documents which are written by eyewitnesses or which reflect their influence are, of course, very important in historical study, if such sources are available. Literary remains in the form of inscriptions in stone, metal or other materials (termed epigraphy) are also available for some types of historical study.

Primary non-literary remains include such objects as material obtained directly from eyewitness interviews, tradition and archaeological artifacts. While direct eyewitness testimony is quite desirable, especially when many such witnesses are available, it is obvious that access to history using this direct type of source cannot go back more than about 100 years, at the most. Then any writings of these eyewitnesses become very valuable sources, as with the American interest of the early 1960s in published interviews with still-living Civil War veterans. Tradition, whether oral or written, can sometimes reach back into antiquity, with devices such as legends, heroic stories or ballads. Americans are familiar with George Washington and the cherry tree or the exploits of Davy Crockett. However, a weakness is that such tradition must be trustworthy and not simply heresay. Reliable tradition based on eyewitness testimony would be an important source. Archaeological artifacts are very valuable witnesses to our past. Remains such as architecture, monuments, gravesites, burial chambers, furniture, artwork, clothes, coins, tools or other implements can often help determine historical background, as well as events. For example, Jewish burial chambers have revealed data concerning burial customs, some average physical characteristics, as well as various types of death inflicted by enemies. Excavations of Qumran near the Dead Sea have uncovered numerous facts concerning the ascetic and communal lifestyle of the sectarian Essenes at about the time of Jesus. Likewise, excavations of Greek cities such as Athens, Corinth and Ephesus have provided invaluable evidence concerning the art, religious beliefs and lifestyle of the Greek culture.

Secondary sources in the form of works such as textbooks, monographs, edited volumes and syllabi witness to primary sources. As such, they help elucidate and expand these previously existing materials.[18]

Even after the historian has his primary and secondary sources, he does not automatically conclude that he has all of the facts. Rather, these sources must be methodologically gathered, organized and criticized before conclusions can be drawn.[19] After gathering all of the materials with which to investigate the topic at hand, the historian will want to have some system of organization by which he can arrange the sources in a preliminary fashion. Then these materials must be checked out by the methods of historical criticism before the claims can be considered as factually valid. Such criticism of written documents, for example, is both external and internal.

External criticism has the purpose of checking out the document itself. Higher criticism judges the authenticity of the writing with regard to its background, authorship, date of writing, where it was written from, to whom it was written and for what reason. Lower criticism concerns the question of whether we have, for all intent and purposes, the original writing as composed. It concerns questions of manuscript evidence, dates of these manuscripts with regard to the original, as well as issues of any documentary interpolations or omissions.

If the historian has found that the documents were indeed written by the claimed author (where one is named), an exact or approximate date, and the fact that we have virtually the same text as originally composed, then internal criticism can begin. The object here is to assess such factors as the competence of the author, the document's reliability and to separate fact from feeling, opinion and other subjective distortion.

Criticism of non-documentary sources could take such forms as the use of dating methods, comparisons to written accounts and even other scientific testing procedures such as chemical analysis. The testing of eyewitness and tradition would follow lines of criticism closer to that used for documentary sources, complete with external and internal phases, such as the date of the testimony, its credibility, and whether it has been modified by time or circumstances.

After the historian gathers and organizes his sources, then applies external and internal criticism, he is ready to formulate his conclusions. The results should conform to all of the known data and provide the most comprehensive and probable judgment on the issues. These results would then be open to careful scrutiny from other scholars, which should cause the careful historian to be modest in his conclusions and able to defend the results, based on the factual data available.

C. Historical research and miracle-claims

Having briefly provided the basis for investigation through the use of historical sources and methodology, we now pose an important question for the Christian apologist. Can miracle-*claims* be examined historically?

Initially, it should be observed that no occurrences can be ruled out *a priori*, unless one can claim to have an omniscient vantage point. In other words, to deny a historical investigation for miracles is to know, in advance, what can or cannot occur. If such was a proper methodology, then any events could be similarly ruled out without so much as an examination.

Some, usually revealing the influence of David Hume, claim that the laws of nature invalidate miracles. This charge is based on several counts of faulty reasoning. Such objections have themselves been refuted on a number of occasions by philosophers and apologists, and cannot be entertained at this point.[20] Most crucially, these hypotheses fail to realize that the major question is not how strong the laws of nature are but if there is a God who has entered history by superseding these very laws in performing a miracle by a superior power. Additionally, modern inductive methodology demands a fair look at all of the relevant historical and philosophical evidence before a conclusion is drawn.

Twentieth century science has changed much from the Enlightenment period, which often spoke in terms of absolutes in nature. But modern science realizes that we can only speak in terms of probabilities. And since we cannot decide in advance what *can* happen, miracles cannot be ruled out *a priori*, and such claims must be investigated. On this subject Montgomery asserts:

> But can the modern man accept a 'miracle' such as the resurrection? ...For us, unlike people of the Newtonian epoch, the universe is no longer a tight, safe, predictable playing-field in which we know all the rules. Since Einstein no modern man has had the right to rule out the possibility of events because of prior knowledge of 'natural law.'[21]

Confirming this view, eminent German physicist Werner Schaaffs has recently argued that the changing view of science causes us to investigate events. Even miracles cannot be rejected without such examination.[22]

As already mentioned, correct inductive research methodology also demands an investigation of all relevant data before conclusions are drawn. This method is used widely, and not just in modern physics. A lawyer is required to review the facts of a specific case before arguing in favor of a conclusion. In medicine, a cure for a disease is announced only after many attempts at gathering data and performing experiments to explain the symptoms in question. In our criminal justice system, a felon is convicted only after an intense analysis where all relevant facts have been carefully weighed. Readers expect journalists to sift through the facts in order to properly present an issue to the public. In these examples and in many others, inductive gathering of evidence is required and is often held to be the best means of gaining data.

Therefore, it is no surprise that historians also make much use of the inductive method of gathering all of the relevant data before a conclusion is rendered. The conviction that probability is the guide to historical (as well as scientific) matters causes induction to be a primary stress in investigations of the facts.

However, the objection is often raised that miracles cannot be analyzed historically. Initially, it should be mentioned that judgments will not be made in this book as to whether miracles have actually occurred. This question involves the complicated philosophical issues of whether this is a theistic universe and if God has chosen to act. Thus, there is a limit in this study with regard to our examination of the resurrection of Jesus. We will investigate its nature as a historical event—if it occurred in history or not. In other words, what evidence is there that Jesus was seen alive by eyewitnesses after he was known to have died? This is a historical issue, for if it literally happened in history, as is often claimed, then it can be investigated. But, for the purposes of this study, we will not inquire into the possibility that the resurrection is a miracle performed by God in a theistic universe.

For these reasons, we can investigate the *historical side* of the miracle-claim that Jesus was raised from the dead without deciding in this present work whether it was actually a miracle. The distinction is thereby being made between the historical portion of a *claim* about a miracle and a demonstrated miracle, which involves philosophical considerations along with the historical ones.

The reader should not decide that one can never reach a conclusion as to whether a certain claim or event is an actual miracle. It is certainly possible (and even desirable) to combine the philosophical study along with the historical inquiry. It is simply not the purpose of this book to present such an analysis.[23]

If the objection is still raised that such claims cannot be studied historically, it should be remembered that such a stance is often related to the original *a priori* rejection raised above. We simply do not know in advance that a miracle could not have occurred, and such a charge therefore cannot be made. If Jesus died, then we can investigate the claims that he appeared alive again to eyewitnesses. Whether it happened or not, such a claim is open to historical examination, especially when the issue of its possibly miraculous nature is not being analyzed here. The critical response should be to attempt to disprove the facts, not to simply ignore them.

In words directed at the historical skepticism of theologian Van Harvey, who argued that we cannot accept the New Testament accounts of the empty tomb even though there is much historical evidence in favor of them and no convincing evidence to the contrary, Wand asserts:

> We may well ask Harvey how a critical historian can do anything else than decide on the evidence before him—unless indeed he already holds some secret which will invalidate in advance any evidence that can be brought in favour of the phenomenon in question? The plain fact is that in this kind of argument the skeptic is not functioning as a historian at all. He starts with the assumption that there could be no corporeal resurrection since that would be against nature....That is to say, he rejects the evidence because he does not like a conclusion that it may be used to support.[24]

What else can the historian do except investigate the available evidence and make a decision based on it?

Sometimes the objection is that miracle-claims are items of faith and that faith cannot be factually investigated. This is a favorite plea from contemporary critical theologians who somehow see faith destroyed by any such analysis of fact. The truth is that earliest Christianity *claimed* that the resurrection of Jesus was an actual space-time, historical fact (1 Cor. 15:3-11) upon which all of Christian theology is based (vv. 12-20). Since it is claimed that it is an actual historical fact, then a historical investigation is possible. We thus find that it is not an investigation of the resurrection that disallows faith, but the view that asserts that Christian faith is separated from history, for it masquerades as the view of early Christians when it plainly is not.

Additionally, if faith is not based on facts (such as the gospel), how can one know that such belief is placed in a trustworthy source? Eternal consequences are at stake and correct choices need to be made. Views which minimize the basing of faith on the historical gospel usually also minimize the gospel itself. But if such facts are true, faith can be exercised. Faith absolutely does not require sight and is not simply a rational exercise, but it does need to be based on the facts of the gospel in order to be both biblical (1 Cor. 15:1-3) and to have a solid foundation.

Our goal, then, is to look at the data and delineate, based on the evidence, historical facts concerning the life, death and resurrection of Jesus. While inspecting the historical side of a miracle-claim such as the resurrection, we will not in this book pursue the philosophical decision as to whether it is a miracle. We desire to be honest with the data and apply the same rules to the sources for the life of Jesus as historians would apply to any ancient writings.[25]

D. Historians and the resurrection of Jesus

The concept of a historical examination of a miracle-claim is ignored by many, but some historians do support such an investigation. For instance, historian of antiquity Paul Maier asks, "What did happen at dawn on Sunday morning?"[26] and the cognate query, "Can history tell us what *actually* happened on that crucial dawn?"[27] We will pursue his answer in later chapters, as well as some of the historical evidence which exists for the empty tomb and the resurrection of Jesus.[28]

Another historian of antiquity, Edwin Yamauchi similarly asserts, "But what is at issue is whether the Resurrection of Christ is rooted in history as an objective event or is simply a creation of the subjective faith of the disciples."[29] He then proceeds to show that, even though such an event would involve factors other than those of normal, causal historical explanations, if this event occurred in history then it can be investigated according to probability. Yamauchi finds much historical evidence for the resurrection of Jesus.[30] The results of his studies will also be pursued below.

William Wand is another historian who holds that we must at least be willing to investigate all the facts in a miracle-claim. If naturalistic hypotheses are probable, these should be pointed out. However, there may well be times when there is good evidence for a miracle-claim. While history cannot prove such an event to be a supernatural miracle, as we already noted, it still may be able to ascertain that the event probably occurred in history.[31]

Thus, if the resurrection of Jesus really occurred in space-time history, it may possibly have ramifications beyond historical causation alone. However, a claim for its historicity, which is precisely the claim made by the earliest church, would open it up at least partially to historical investigation. These historians agree with such a historical inquiry.

E. Summary and conclusion

Starting with history as both event and record of that event, we have endeavored to note the sources of the historian and his methodology.

Stating such preliminary considerations will lay the groundwork for our discussion of history and miracles.

It was asserted that *a priori* rejections of miracles are invalid. The lack of an omniscient point of judgment, the scientific stress on probabilities and the nature of inductive methodology all validate this conclusion.

Although some object to historical investigations of miracle-claims, it was pointed out that we will only investigate the historical aspect of such claims in this book. The philosophical counterpart will not be dealt with here, although nothing prohibits combining philosophical and historical endeavors in order to determine whether an event is a miracle or not.

This book is concerned with the historical basis for the life, death and resurrection of Jesus. These periods in Jesus' life involve historical issues, since it is claimed that these events happened in literal, space-time history. As such, they can be examined. *A priori* rejections do not change whatever history may reveal. For those who want miracles to remain completely in the area of faith, it should be pointed out that, for the earliest Christians, the resurrection of Jesus was claimed as a space-time, historical fact. Such a claim to be history opens this belief to historical investigation. And if it can be investigated, then miracle-claims can be examined. Faith should not be divorced from history. Several contemporary historians realize this and have called for an investigation of miracle-claims. We wish to conduct just such an examination, utilizing the historical sources and methodology.

Notes

[1] See Patrick Gardiner's articles "The Philosophy of History" in the *International Encyclopedia of the Social Sciences*, ed. by David L. Sills (New York: The Macmillan Company and The Free Press, 1968) vol. 6, pp. 428-433, for some of these interpretations.

[2] W. H. Walsh, *Philosophy of History* (New York: Harper and Brothers, Publishers, 1960), pp. 101, 103.

[3] William Wand, *Christianity: A Historical Religion?* (Valley Forge: Judson Press, 1972), pp. 29, 31, 42; cf. Gardiner, pp. 432-433.

[4] See Moses Hadas' "Introduction" to *The Complete Works of Tacitus* (New York: Random House, Inc., 1942), pp. IX-XVII.

[5] Ibid., p. XIX.

[6] Ibid., p. IX.

[7]Ibid., XVII-XVIII.

[8]Michael Grant, *Jesus: An Historian's Review of the Gospels* (New York: Charles Scribner's Sons, 1977), pp. 183-189.

[9]Ibid.; also Hadas, pp. XVII-XVIII.

[10]Wand, pp. 51-52.

[11]Ernest Nagel, "Determinism in History" in William Dray, editor, *Philosophical Analysis and History* (New York: Harper and Row, Publishers, 1966), p. 355.

[12]Ibid.

[13]Wand, pp. 25-27, 51-52, 156.

[14]John Warwick Montgomery, *Where is History Going?* (Grand Rapids: Zondervan Publishing House, 1969), pp. 71-74.

[15]For a more complete treatment, see Earle E. Cairns, *God and Man in Time* (Grand Rapids: Baker Book House, 1979), pp. 11-29.

[16]Walsh, p. 18. For a good example of such an investigation with regard to ancient historical events, see Delbrück's methods of determining how ancient battles had been fought in the times of the Greek and Roman empires. This scholar was able to arrive at historical facts concerning how large the opposing armies were, how they maneuvered and other such facets of specific battles in ancient times by examining the ancient historical records. For instance, see Edward M. Earle, editor, *Makers of Modern Strategy* (Princeton: Princeton University Press, 1943), especially pp. 264-268 with regard to Delbrück's historical method.

[17]Walsh, pp. 18-19.

[18]For details on the following discussion, see Cairns, pp. 33-42, although we will diverge at certain points.

[19]Ibid., pp. 43-56.

[20]For refutations of David Hume and others, especially those in the twentieth century analytic tradition, see Gary Habermas, "Skepticism: Hume" in *Biblical Errancy: An Analysis of its Philosophical Roots*, ed. by Norman L. Geisler (Grand Rapids: Zondervan Publishing House, 1981), pp. 23-49.

[21]Montgomery, p. 71.

[22]See Werner Schaaffs, *Theology, Physics and Miracles*, transl. by Richard L. Renfield (Washington D.C.: Canon Press, 1974).

[23]For a full examination of the resurrection as an actual miracle, see Gary R. Habermas, *The Resurrection of Jesus: An Apologetic* (Grand Rapids: Baker Book House, 1980).

[24]Wand, *Christianity: Historical Religion?*, pp. 70-71.

[25]See Michael Grant, *Jesus, An Historian's Review*, pp. 199-200, who states that this is a valid procedure.

[26]Paul Maier, *First Easter* (New York: Harper and Row, Publishers, 1973), p. 93.

[27]Ibid., p. 114.

[28]Ibid., especially, pp. 114-122.

[29]Edwin Yamauchi, "Easter—Myth, Hallucination or History?" in *Christianity Today*, March 15, 1974, pp. 4-7 and March 29, 1974, pp. 12-16.
[30]Ibid., March 29, 1974, pp. 12-16.
[31]Wand, *Christianity: Historical Religion?*, pp. 29-31, 51-52, 93-94.

2

Misconceptions Concerning the Historicity of Jesus

A number of objections are sometimes raised concerning the possibility of a historical investigation into the life of Jesus. Such objections range all the way from the few persons who doubt his very historical existence to popularistic attempts to present his life in more or less novelistic form, usually in rather non-historical and subjective fashion.

The purpose of this chapter is to set forth a number of common misconceptions with regard to formulating our historical case for Jesus' life, proceeding generally from the more to the less radical views. Each question will be presented, with an initial critique being given as to its shortcomings. Many criticisms in this chapter anticipate the research which will be presented consequently, which is then followed by additional critiques in light of this research, given in the first Appendix.

A. Did Jesus ever live?

Comparatively few recent scholars postulate that Jesus never lived. Such positions are usually viewed as blatant misuses of the available historical data. Yet this general thesis still appears, as with the recent writings of G. A. Wells,[1] who holds that Jesus may be a historical personage, albeit an obscure one. However, he asserts that it is very possible Jesus never existed at all, but was patterned after ancient mystery religions by the New Testament authors.

A central theme in Wells' writings is the chronological order of the New Testament books. This order is supposed to reveal much Christological development. He finds four stages, the earliest being Paul's epistles, all written before 60 A.D. These are followed by the non-Pauline canonical epistles, the pastoral epistles and non-canonical writings of Ignatius, with the fourth stage being the Gospels. With the exception of Paul's epistles, Wells believes that the rest of these books are rather late.

The last three stages are dated by him between 70 and 120 A.D.

Paul's writings are said to reveal very little knowledge of the historicity of Jesus, since Wells believes that Paul knew virtually no details of Jesus' life, including neither the time of his birth, death nor reported resurrection appearances. Rather, Paul is said to have conceived of Jesus as a supernatural being who led a very obscure life which was ended by crucifixion, perhaps even centuries before Paul's own time. The second stage of New Testament writings, the non-Pauline epistles, denote a slight shift in thinking. They assert that Jesus lived on earth *recently*, an element which Wells believes is absent from Paul altogether. The pastoral epistles and Ignatius' non-canonical writings mark a later stage in the early second century when Jesus is linked with the governorship of Pilate and death at Roman hands. The Gospels represent the fourth stage in which there is an interest in a full history of the life of Jesus, which is more or less fabricated. According to Wells, the early church simply accepted any reconstruction of the life of Jesus which did not conflict with other well-established beliefs. Mark was the earliest gospel (90 A.D.), followed by Matthew and Luke, with John being the last one written (early second century).[2]

With this configuration, Wells concludes that the historical facts of Jesus' life were mostly a late addition to the New Testament, since Paul, the author of the earliest books, was not overly interested in historical details. The earliest Christians stressed not the historical Jesus, but the divine Christ who was little different from the mystery gods of other ancient peoples. In fact, Jewish concepts of wisdom plus influence from the mystery religions helped inspire the early picture of Jesus. It is thereby possible that Jesus never existed at all or, if he did, that he lived a very obscure life and attracted very little attention. At any rate, Christianity got its start, according to Wells, without any contact with a historical Jesus who supposedly died about 30 A.D. Nothing precise is said to have been known about him since no firsthand information is presented in the New Testament.[3]

Of the numerous problems with Wells' thesis, we will mention four major points here. First and possibly most important, the earliest books of the New Testament do exhibit much interest in the life, death and resurrection of the historical Jesus, including the preservation of eyewitness testimony to these facts. It is no coincidence that Paul is the author who includes one of the most important indications of this interest in 1 Cor. 15:3ff., where he incorporates a very early Christian creed which is much older than the book in which it appears. Such early traditions appear frequently in the New Testament and actually consist of oral teachings and proclamations which were repeated by word of mouth until recorded in the book itself. Therefore these creeds actually predate the New Testament writings in which they occur. This creed reports the death, burial and resurrection of Jesus, relating that he rose the third day after he was killed. A list of persons to whom he appeared then follows.

This creed links the historical life of Jesus (vv. 3-4) with those eyewitnesses who testified to his resurrection appearances beginning on the third day after his death (vv. 5-7). In addition, Paul had not only met some of these witnesses personally (Gal. 1:18-19; 2:9), but he explains that his message concerning these facts is identical with their eyewitness testimony (1 Cor. 15:11; cf. 14, 15). The eyewitnesses of Jesus, and especially of his resurrection, were relating the same facts as Paul. Also of crucial importance, this creed is very close to the events themselves, and therefore cannot be dismissed as late material or as hearsay evidence. Critics not only admit this data, but were the first ones who recognized the early date.

Paul even goes as far as to say that if these historical facts concerning Jesus' resurrection are not true, then there is absolutely no grounds whatsoever for the Christian faith (1 Cor. 15:12-19, 32). (See further Chapter V.) This early creed and the subsequent testimony alone disprove Wells' thesis, for they demonstrate clearly that Paul is basing the Christian faith on the historical facts of Jesus' recent life, death and resurrection.

Wells admits that his position depends on the ability to assert that Christianity could have started without a historical Jesus who had lived recently,[4] but this is exactly where his thesis is the weakest. Paul bases his entire message on the truthfulness of these facts, in addition to presenting eyewitness testimony to further corroborate these recent events from witnesses which he both knows personally and with whom his own message agrees. That this creed is also very early and close to the events themselves, further substantiates the testimony, as does the probability that the testimony is accurate. Other portions of Paul's writings confirm this conclusion, in opposition to Wells.

Paul's references to Cephas and the twelve (1 Cor. 15:5), to the apostles, brothers of Christ and Cephas (1 Cor. 9:5) and James as the brother of the Lord in the same context as the apostle Peter (Gal. 1:18-19) are examples of Paul's knowledge of Jesus' contemporaries, further revealing that he lived recently. Again, their connection to Jesus by the phrase "the third day" (1 Cor. 15:3-4) solidifies this view. Wells' explanation of these texts is insufficient, as well as faulty.[5] He provides a good example here of the logical fallacy known as "pettifogging," but raising a smoke screen about some of these phrases is not the same as removing all historical reference to the earthly ministry of Jesus. We may not like what the texts state but we cannot thereby cause Jesus and his contemporaries to disappear simply by this type of *reductio ad absurdum*. Virtually all New Testament scholars realize that the New Testament has many references, such as these above, to some of the persons who knew Jesus during his recent ministry. While Paul's epistles certainly do not contain much of the detail of the Gospels, to be sure, there is no reason to claim that he was largely disinterested. An impressive compilation of facts concerning Jesus and his ministry, learned from persons who knew Jesus, can be built from these epistles of Paul alone.[6] Since the epistles of Paul are, for Wells, the most crucial material in this regard, we have an important indication of his failure at this point.

A second major problem in Wells' thesis is his late-dating of the Gospels, in conjunction with his belief that no New Testament source prior to 90 A.D. links the death of Jesus with Pilate. Such dates for the Gospels may have been popular in the nineteenth century, but are abandoned today by the vast majority of critical scholars. Although it is not in the scope of this book to take an indepth look at the dates of the Gospels, even most critical scholars date Mark about 65 A.D., and Matthew and Luke about 80 A.D., which is about twenty to twenty-five years earlier than Wells' dates. John is usually dated at the end of the first century (90-100 A.D.), not in the second century. Some even accept dates earlier than these, but virtually all critical biblical scholars differ with Wells' data.[7] Even historians such as Michael Grant accept the earlier dates, again contrary to Wells' view.[8]

At any rate, Wells' assertion that the New Testament does not link Jesus with Pilate prior to 90 A.D. is in error, as is the ridiculous line of reasoning by which Wells believes the early church unanimiously chose Pilate's name—because he was the kind of person who would crucify Jesus, even though he did not! He obviously prefers such a thesis because it facilitates his four-stage development of the New Testament. Yet his view is not compelling because it conflicts with the facts, as reflected by the majority of critical scholars who disagee with him.

A third criticism follows as a result of the second. Wells' assertion that the lateness of the Gospels caused its writers to do much guessing and accepting as "fact" anything that did not conflict with their general framework, also fails. Since the Gospels are much earlier than he postulates, they are much closer to the events which they record. They could be controlled by eyewitness testimony and thereby point strongly to the reliability of the material.[9]

Such a thesis follows much more coherently from the earlier dating of the Gospels at a time when eyewitnesses were still alive. And the evidence does indicate that the Gospels yield historically reliable material about Jesus. Historian Michael Grant specificaly notes that this is the major problem with Wells' thesis:

> But, above all, if we apply to the New Testament, as we should, the same sort of criteria as we should apply to other ancient writings containing historical material, we can no more reject Jesus' existence than we can reject the existence of a mass of pagan personages whose reality as historical figures is never questioned.[10]

By normal historical standards which are used to ascertain other events in ancient history, we can learn about Jesus as well.

The fourth major problem with Wells' approach concerns his usage of the ancient mystery religions to explain the early Christian worship of Jesus. Again, such a reliance on legends was a popular thesis in times past, but has been dismissed today by most researchers.

Two refutations of this legend theory have already been mentioned above. Paul's use of the creed in 1 Cor. 15:3ff. reveals that the proclamation of Jesus' death and resurrection was both early and dependent on *eyewitnesses*. As Pannenberg concludes:

> Under such circumstances it is an idle venture to make parallels in the history of religions responsible for the *emergence* of the primitive Christian message about Jesus' resurrection.[11]

It was the disciples who had these actual experiences and that rules out such a mythical theory since the original teaching of the resurrection is based on real eyewitness experiences and not on later legends.

Other problems also abound with such a theory, examples of which can only be briefly mentioned here. It is common for the similarities in these mystery religions to be mentioned without also noting the great differences. Wells notes the pagan mythical deities who were believed to have returned to life on the third day, without mentioning those believed to have regained life on the first, second or fourth days.[12] Even Otto Pfleiderer, an advocate of the mythical thesis many years ago, admits that this is a valid criticism and points out that differences must also be stressed.[13]

Additionally, there is no case of a mythical deity in the mystery religions for which we have both clear and early evidence that a resurrection was taught prior to the late second century A.D. Thus, it is certainly a plausible thesis that the mystery religions borrowed this aspect from Christianity, not the reverse.[14]

Lastly, scholars now realize that there was very little influence from the mystery religions in first century Palestine at all. Michael Grant notes this as another major problem with Wells' thesis. "Judaism was a milieu to which doctrines of the deaths and rebirths of mythical gods seems so entirely foreign that the emergence of such a fabrication from its midst is very hard to credit."[15] Other scholars agree with this assessment.[16]

Virtually no writers have asserted that Jesus did not exist or have attempted to cast virtually total doubt and obscurity on his life and ministry. But, such efforts are refuted by the early and eyewitness testimony presented by Paul and others, by the early date of the Gospels, by the corresponding historicity and trustworthiness of the Gospels, and by the failure of the mystery religions to explain the Christian faith.

While very few persons support a thesis such as Wells', other skeptical views attract more followers. We will now turn to the major representatives.

B. We can know little about the historical Jesus

Very few scholars hold the view that Jesus never lived. Even Rudolf Bultmann, one of the most influential critical theologians of the twentieth century and exponent of demythologizing the Scripture, said, "By no means are we at the mercy of those who doubt or deny that Jesus ever lived."[17]

More popular, especially from about 1930-1960, is the view that the Gospels do not purport to record actual historical events, but that they simply report the faith of early Christians. We thereby find in the Gospels not a historical record, but a witness to early Christian belief. Accordingly, we know much less about the historical Jesus than the

Gospels actually record, for these writers were just not overly concerned with history. This view was popularized by Bultmann, who held that the Gospels are essentially a later interpretation of Jesus' person and teachings, largely in mythical terms. This interpretation emerged from the viewpoint of a post-Easter faith which freely modified the historical Jesus into a partially mythical figure. According to this theory, the gospel writers attempted to utilize imagery in order to express spiritual concepts in terms of this world. As an example, God's transcendence might be described as immense spatial distance. Often supernatural imagery might be used, perhaps by picturing God's control of nature with a miracle, which was believed to reveal His omnipotence. Such mythical expressions were said to be literally meaningless today. Therefore, Bultmann attempted to demythologize the Gospels by ascertaining what the writers were really trying to communicate and by reinterpreting it into a message which is existentially valid for twentieth century humanity.[18]

For example, Bultmann's treatment of the resurrection of Jesus is accomplished without a historical investigation of any sort. He concludes at the very outset, "Is it not a mythical event pure and simple? Obviously it is not an event of past history."[19] While the faith which the earliest disciples had in Jesus' resurrection is a historical fact, it is not even important to know the cause for this faith.[20] Thus, the historicity of the resurrection is rejected *a priori* as a myth, without any attempt to investigate the facts. Even the importance of such historical research is rejected. Because the early church is said not to have been interested in recording history, legend was mixed into the gospel accounts in particular. As a result, Bultmann postulated that there is much uncertainty as to the historical aspects of Jesus' life and teachings.[21]

In his earlier writings, Bultmann expressed this conclusion quite strongly, such as his belief that "we can know almost nothing concerning the life and personality of Jesus.[22] To be sure, Bultmann does accept a number of historical facts concerning the life and message of Jesus, especially in his later writings.[23] We will present a list of such facts accepted by historical skeptics in Chapter V, where Bultmann's treatment will be a focus.

While the works of Rudolf Bultmann are probably the best known source for the position which holds that little can be known about the historical Jesus, other critics have also held this view as well, including a number of his disciples. However, the influence of his work has been declining in the last twenty years. There are numerous reasons for the more recent decline in Bultmann's popularity for this, but important points will be raised.

First, the major problem in terms of this study is that he dismisses the historicity of Jesus' resurrection without any investigation at all. Rather than consider the evidence, he rejects it *a priori*. Even John Macquarrie, who is perhaps the most eminent commentator on Bultmann's thought, sharply criticizes him on this point:

> And here we must take Bultmann to task for what appears to be an en-tirely arbitrary dismissal of the possibility of understanding the resurrec-tion as an objective-historical event....The fallacy of such reasoning is obvious. The one valid way in which we can ascertain whether a certain event took place or not is not by bringing in some sweeping assumption to show that it could not have taken place, but to consider the historical evidence available, and decide on that.[24]

The problem is that Bultmann makes his decision against the facticity of the resurrection apart from factual observation. Again, in the words of Macquarrie:

> But Bultmann does not take the trouble to examine what evidence could be adduced to show that the resurrection was an objective-historical event. He assumes that it is myth.[25]

Therefore, the facts that could be enough to demonstrate the historical resurrection are ignored by Bultmann. Interestingly enough, it will even be pointed out below how this methodology of radical form criticism, which he popularized, even backfired into an argument for miracle-claims.

The second problem with Bultmann's approach is that, by his usage of only a minimum historical basis in the life of Jesus, he fails to provide both early and modern Christians with the factual grounding which is indispensable for the founding and present existence of the Christian faith. For instance, the New Testament often claims to be based on his-torically accurate accounts.[26] Indeed, Paul even asserts that, apart from a historical gospel, there is no basis for faith whatsoever, since it would be vain and groundless (1 Cor. 15:1-20). The main point here is not an *a priori* rejection of Bultmann's approach, but the assertion that without a known historical core of knowledge about Jesus, Christianity would have had no initial impetus to encourage faith in an otherwise unknown Jesus.

It is this criticism that is probably the single most influential contribution to the current dissatisfaction with this theologian's system of thought. It is Macquarrie, who, while supporting Bultmann in a number of points, again takes issue with him here:

> It is very doubtful whether the Christian faith could have been built upon the foundation of a historic Jesus who, as Bultmann presents him, was little more than a teacher of a practical philosophy with certain resemblances to existentialism, and who is stripped of the numinous characteristics which the Gospels ascribe to him.[27]

At present, most of Bultmann's disciples disagree with their mentor over this very point, when asserting that there must be some adequate historical knowledge of Jesus. Thus, while these "new quest for the historical Jesus" scholars do not stress these historical facts as the basis for faith, they do hold that, without such, violence is done both to the apostolic *kerygma* (the kernel of their message) and to the present understanding of Jesus.[28] Bultmann has apparently been affected by some of these critiques, since in his later years he admitted more historical knowledge about Jesus.[29] Christianity proclaimed a historical basis for its message. If an investigation reveals that such a basis exists, then these facts must have a more important function than Bultmann allows.

The third problem in Bultmann's approach is that even historians of antiquity oppose the specific version of form and redaction criticism that he popularized as the proper methodological approach to New Testament studies. Whereas Bultmann's usage of these methods revealed the minimal historical results noted above, ancient historians have employed their normal patterns of investigation and found an adequate basis for history in the New Testament. Oxford historian of antiquity A. N. Sherwin-White levelled the following indictment at form critics:

> So, it is astonishing that while Graeco-Roman historians have been growing in confidence, the twentieth-century study of the Gospel narratives, starting from no less promising material, has taken so gloomy a turn in the development of form-criticism...that the historical Christ is unknowable and the history of his mission cannot be written. This seems very curious.[30]

Sherwin-White points out that the same standards which are commonly applied to ancient secular history can also be applied to the New Testament records, with the result that a factual account emerges. Another renowned historian of antiquity, Michael Grant, likewise applies the techniques of normal historical methodology to the New Testament and also concludes that much can be known about the historical Jesus, in spite of the efforts of Bultmann, whose methodology Grant specifically rejects.[31]

Here an objection is often raised. It is sometimes asserted that the New Testament authors cannot be compared to ancient historians, since the latter were writing history while form-critics hold that the former allowed their beliefs to significantly color their recording. To this question and to the larger issue of the form criticism advocated by Bultmann, Sherwin-White and Grant provide numerous responses. (1) There are several examples of well-known ancient historians whose works are quite similar to the author's intention and methodology in the Gospels, "which the evangelists would have applauded," yet they are well accepted as historical.[32] (2) Literature like the form-critics believe the Gospels to be is not known elsewhere in ancient history. As Sherwin-White asserts, "We are not acquainted with this type of writing in ancient historiography."[33]

(3) The Gospels are quite close to the period of time which they record, while ancient histories often describe events which took place centuries earlier. Yet, modern historians are able to successfully derive the events even from these ancient periods of time. (4) Ancient histories sometimes "disagree amongst themselves in the widest possible fashion," yet the history they record can still be ascertained.[34]

(5) Form-critics speak much of the experiences of the earliest disciples, but history looks for adequate causes behind these experiences. (6) The New Testament, such as the book of Acts, is confirmed by external guarantees of historicity. (7) The principles of form criticism do not preclude an important place for history in the Gospels. Although the primary interest of the gospel writers was spiritual, history was also very important. There is no good reason why they would pervert the historical in order to preserve the spiritual, when both were so important and complimented one another.

Sherwin-White and Grant are examples of historians who have pointed out some of the many weaknesses in the form-critical method as espoused by Bultmann.[35] Both scholars conclude that if the same criteria which are applied to other ancient writings are applied to the New Testament, we can delineate a historical basis for the life and teachings of Jesus.[36]

Our fourth critique again concerns the form-critical approach to the Gospels as represented by Bultmann. Not only do these books present a good historical basis, as noted by historians, but they are also shown to be trustworthy documents when judged according to their manuscript evidence, as witnessed by many critical theologians.

Concerning the question of manuscript evidence, the New Testament is easily the best attested ancient writing in terms of the number of manuscripts, the period of time between writing and the earliest copy and the completeness of the whole. Ancient classical works have comparatively few manuscripts, with twenty entire or partial copies generally being an excellent number. By comparison, the New Testament has over 5000 munuscripts or partial copies. Such a wide difference would provide the New Testament with a much better means of textual criticism in ascertaining the original text.[37]

Perhaps the strongest manuscript evidence concerns the date between the original and the earliest copy. For most of the ancient classical works, a gap of between 700 and 1400 years is very common. By comparison, the Chester Beatty Papyri contain most of the New Testament and are dated about 100-150 years after its completion. A complete copy of the New Testament (Codex Sinaiticus) and a nearly complete manuscript (Codex Vaticanus) date only about 250 years after the original autographs. Such early dates for the New Testament help to insure its authenticity.[38]

Additionally, while we have the entire New Testament text, it is not so with all other ancient works. For instance, of the 142 books of Roman history written by Livy, 107 books have been lost. Only four and a half of Tacitus' original fourteen books of Roman *Histories* remain in existence and only ten full and two partial books remain from Tacitus' sixteen books of his *Annals*. Not only is each book in complete form, we also have complete copies of all of the New Testament books. This is also a factor in establishing the authenticity of these writings.[39] Also, each New Testament book is complete.

Other critiques could be raised against Bultmann's form-critical approach to the Gospels. For instance, some have noted his outdated, nineteenth century view of science which causes him to refer to anything which does not fit his system as "myth."[40] Others note that he is also dated in his heavy reliance on Hellenistic influences for much of New Testament teaching, instead of turning to the now demonstrated Jewish milieu.[41] One serious claim is that his lack of emphasis on the historicity of Jesus qualifies his system as a type of twentieth century gnosticism.[42] Some even believe that Bultmann's lack of stress on the historical Jesus leaves him in the precarious position of having to demythologize Jesus himself in order to be logical.[43]

Nonetheless, the four major critiques against Bultmann and others who employ radical form and redaction criticism serve to refute this approach to the historicity of Jesus. The improper and *a priori* dismissal of supernatural events such as the resurrection, the lack of an adequate historical basis required for early Christian faith, the historical problems with radical form criticism and the trustworthiness of the New Testament texts invalidate this approach. Other efforts to minimize the historical facts in the life of Jesus also fall prey to these criticisms. With a historical basis, Jesus' life and teachings can be reconstructed.

C. A historical Jesus without theology or miracles

A less radical but very popular model for pursuing history in the life of Jesus is to accept the Gospels as fairly reliable historical records, and then produce an outline of his life from them, usually ignoring the miraculous and the theological portions of the material. This approach is appealing to Michael Grant, who judges that, while much history can be gained by such a method, the miraculous elements in the life of Jesus are not within the purview of the historian, but are in the realm of faith.[44] Nevertheless, Grant does find a considerable amount of history in the life of Jesus.[45]

In addition to historians, this approach of ascertaining historical facts from the Gospels was made famous by the theological movement known as nineteenth century liberalism. Often termed "old liberalism" to distinguish it from other modernistic alternatives, the chief methodology was to reconstruct Jesus' life chiefly by using the synoptic Gospels. These sources were viewed as quite adequate materials for this endeavor, with the general exceptions of doctrinal portions and miracles. In other words, the old liberals usually accepted the facts presented in the synoptic Gospels, but endeavored to get to the man behind the early theological creeds and to provide naturalistic explanations for the miracles.[46]

On the one hand, the doctrinal affirmation of Jesus being both divine and human was viewed by these liberals as being untenable, so their desire was to "unmask" the historical Jesus from the Christ of faith and doctrine. They attempted to strip the Christ of dogma from the human Jesus.[47] On the other hand, miracles were also seen as untenable. Therefore, accounts containing them were usually accepted as presenting true scenarios and true facts, minus the actual miraculous portion. This element was explained by normal (naturalistic) phenomena. For example, in the early nineteenth century, Heinrich Paulus accepted most of the gospel reports surrounding the death and resurrection of Jesus with one major exception: Jesus was said to have been removed from the cross while he was still alive. The resulting explanation accepted most of the facts but attempted to remove the supernatural explanation of the resurrection.[48]

This approach presents some seemingly compelling ideas, such as viewing the Gospels as generally historical sources, an attitude which takes the supporting evidence and historical data seriously. However, there are several reasons why it falls short, and this led to the rejection of old liberalism. We will present four major critiques of this view.

First, many have questioned the assumption that we can accept part of the gospel record and reject part of it *a priori* according to one's own standards of value. Such picking and choosing is surely arbitrary unless there is some valid criteria for determining that which is accepted and that which is rejected. Why should miracles be rejected, unless we have prior knowledge that they can *never* be factually valid? Neither history, science nor any other discipline can rule out miracles without an investigation. The claim that miracles are contrary to the laws of nature and therefore invalid is itself based on faulty reasoning and thus cannot rule out miracles *a priori*.[49]

Current science is in a state where we are no longer able to postulate absolutes which can rule out events *a priori*, as was often believed possible in the Enlightenment period. We can therefore only speak in terms of probabilities for any given occurrence. Even more important, the technique of examining all of the evidence before conclusions are drawn is required by correct inductive research methodology. Accordingly, such an approach is utilized not only in physics, but in such varied disciplines as law, medical science, criminal justice and journalism. Historians also investigate the known facts to find whether an event actually happened or not. (See Chapter I.)

As former Oxford lecturer William Wand remarks, there is no scholarly reason for rejecting possibilities before just such an investigation. An *a priori* dismissal cannot be allowed, even if we do not like the conclusion which is indicated by the facts. One must decide on the known evidence.[50]

For these reasons, conclusions which are drawn before and against the facts are both non-historical and non-scientific. Therefore, to rule out the possibility of miracles *a priori* is not a valid procedure. We must investigate the evidence and then draw conclusions.

The second major problem with this approach is the common assumption (also raised in Chapter I) that miracle-claims cannot be investigated by historical methodology at all. Often the charge is made that miracles belong in the realm of religious faith and, as such, are out of the reach of the tools of historical or any other investigation.

It should be repeated that it is not the purpose of this book to determine if a miracle has occurred. All that we purport to do in this book is to investigate the life of Jesus in general, and his resurrection in particular, according to historical standards.

For such a philosophical and historical investigation of the resurrection as an actual miracle caused by God, which is an entirely appropriate study, the interested reader is referred to the author's book *The Resurrection of Jesus: An Apologetic.*[51]

As indicated in Chapter I, we are distinguishing between a miracle-*claim* and a miracle. We can therefore historically investigate the Christian claim that Jesus was raised from the dead without raising the attendant question in this present study of whether it is a miracle caused by God in a theistic universe. Nonetheless, the historical question of the historicity of the resurrection is quite important even by itself, for *if* a miracle did literally occur, it needs the historical attestation as well. Our direction will thus be to examine the historical side of the claim that Jesus was raised. Did Jesus, after dying on the cross by crucifixion, appear to his followers alive? This is our major focus.

Therefore, the charge that historical methodology cannot take us all the way to the conclusion that a miracle has actually occurred is a valid concern. However, this is entirely different from the assertion that historical inquiry is thereby incorrect. But we need to distinguish between these two aspects. The original charge, then, that miracles cannot be investigated, would only be correct if we knew in advance that miracles do not literally occur in history. If they happen only in some non-objective personal realm or if they do not occur at all, then they cannot be investigated by historical methodology and this is a correct assessment. However, since the claim that miracles literally occur in normal history is an open question, then it would at least be possible to investigate the historical portion of these claims as to their validity or invalidity.

While some will object that even a partial investigation of a miracle-*claim* is in any sense still impossible, such an assertion is often simply a form of *a priori* objection just answered in the first critique above. In other words, since we cannot rule out the possibility of miracles *a priori*, and since it is claimed that miracles have happened in space-time history, they can be investigated as such.

For those who object to investigations of any sort with regard to miracle-claims, holding that they are only tenets of faith, it must be remembered that the New Testament teaches that the resurrection is an event of actual, space-time history (1 Cor. 15:1-20, for instance). If it is found that there is demonstrable historical evidence for the resurrection, this would be the final indication that this event can be investigated historically—for it obviously can be examined. Although many ignore these issues, some historians have called for just such an investigation. They hold that any evidence for the resurrection must be examined. Then we can judge whether it is an actual event of history.[52]

This same portion of Scripture just mentioned also states that salvation consists of trust in the facts of the Gospel, including Jesus' resurrection (vv. 1-4). Paul asserts that faith is built on these firm facts. As stated earlier, if faith is not placed in a trustworthy source, how can we know that it is valid at all? Again, we do not need sight as a basis for faith, but historical facts provide a stronger foundation for faith than does a hopeful "leap."

A third problem with this approach to history in the life of Jesus, especially with old liberalism, is that the naturalistic theories which were proposed to account for the resurrection were disproven by the known historical facts. Interestingly enough, it was the liberals themselves who attacked their own theories, in spite of their presuppositions.

These naturalistic views were very popular in the nineteenth century. There was no consensus of opinion on which theory was the best alternative explanation for the literal resurrection. In fact, many of those who popularized these theories did so only after attacking and revealing the weaknesses in the other theories of fellow liberals. For instance, Paulus' "swoon theory" mentioned above was disarmed by David Strauss, who, according to Schweitzer, dealt it its "death-blow."[53] (See

Chapter III for an in-depth study of this theory.)

It is not the purpose of this book to take an in-depth look at these alternative theories proposed to explain away the facticity of Jesus' resurrection. Suffice it to remark here that, as with Paulus' theory, each of the naturalistic theories was disproven by the liberals themselves. By this process, and by the critiques of others outside their camp, the weaknesses of these attempts were revealed. In other words, each of the alternative theories were disproven by the known historical facts.[54]

It is also instructive to note that twentieth century critics usually rejected these theories wholesale. Thus, rather than deal with each proposition separately, the naturalistic attempts to disprove the resurrection were generally dismissed in their entirety by recent critical scholars. For example, Karl Barth, probably the most influential critical theologian of this century, listed the major naturalistic theories and concluded that "Today we rightly turn our nose up at this," a conclusion derived at least partially from "the many inconsistencies in detail." He also notes that these explanations "have now gone out of currency."[55] Similarly, Raymond Brown also provides a list of these theories and then concludes: "the criticism of today does not follow the paths taken by criticism in the past. No longer respectable are the crude theories...popular in the last century."[56] These are just examples of the many contemporary critical theologians who have rejected the alternative theories against the resurrection.[57]

Therefore, not only were the naturalistic theories disproven by the historical facts, but nineteenth century liberals critiqued these views individually, while twentieth century critics have generally dismissed these alternative theories as a whole. As such, we have an important indication of the failure of this approach to the history in Jesus' life, since it falls short at such a crucial point.

The fourth critique of this historical approach will only be mentioned briefly since it cannot be dealt with in this book. But the attempt of both contemporary historians and nineteenth century liberals alike to ignore the theological teachings in the life of Jesus might also be subject to revision if it is found that Jesus did, in fact, rise from the dead.[58] To be sure, theology is not in the purview of history and this is the major reason it is not dealt with in history books. But this cannot be said of the nineteenth century liberal theologians. If the resurrection were shown to be an historical event, it would have much possible relevance for theology. Therefore, theology cannot be ruled out as irrelevant.

We must therefore rule out this final option as an invalid attempt to pursue a study of history in the life of Christ. It fails in that it usually rejects the possibility of miracles in an *a priori* manner, but also because it often rejects any investigation of miracle-claims at all. Additionally, its naturalistic approach to Jesus' resurrection has failed, as even critics admit, and it also ignores the possibility that, if Jesus literally arose from the dead, then there is certainly a possible relevance for theology.

D. No extra-New Testament sources for Jesus

The last view which we will examine in this chapter is the often-mentioned opinion that everything which we know about Jesus is recorded in the New Testament, and the Gospels in particular. These are said to be our *only* sources for the life of Jesus, since ancient history knows nothing of him.

Actually, this view is distinct from the other approaches which we have set forth, since it is compatible with any number of possible positions with regard to the historicity of Jesus, including the three other views set forth in this chapter. On the other hand, it need not be a critical theory at all, in that some believers hold the view that the uniqueness of Jesus is increased because of their belief that only Christian records know of his teaching and life. Sometimes this position is held as a challenge to Christians, since some pose the question that if Jesus made such an impact on the people of his time, then why do we know nothing of him from ancient history?

Whatever the motivation or belief of the one holding this opinion, it certainly is held by a seemingly wide spectrum of persons. As one historian of antiquity asserts:

> Historical information about the beginnings of Christianity is unfortunately very limited. No external source, Jewish or classical, records the career of Jesus, and our entire knowledge comes from the subsequent writings of his followers gathered together in the *Gospels*. Modern scholarship no longer doubts the authenticity of these writings[59] (emphasis added by author).

The authors certainly do not sound overly critical and perhaps they are speaking of a fully developed life of Jesus in ancient history. Nevertheless, this view is echoed by many persons. Consider the words of a fictitious archaeologist in a modern novel who is very skeptical of Christianity:

> The church bases its claims mostly on the teachings of an obscure young Jew with messianic pretensions who, let's face it, didn't make much of an impression in his lifetime. There isn't a single word about him in secular history. Not a word. No mention of him by the Romans. Not so much as a reference by Josephus.[60]

Although the character who uttered this pronouncement is fictitious, the charge is a frequent one and, as in this case, sometimes used in an attempt to discredit Christianity. We will simply make two responses to this view here, especially since it is not necessarily a critical attempt to discredit the pursuit of the historical Jesus.

First, it is simply false to hold that there are no ancient sources outside of the New Testament which speak of Jesus. It is true that none of these extra-biblical sources gives a detailed account concerning Jesus, but there are nevertheless well over a dozen non-Christian sources from ancient history which mention him. There are also a number of early Christian sources which give more information concerning him. We will have to wait until Part Two to specifically substantiate this claim, but it is enough here to note that it is incorrect to assert that the ancient non-Christian world knew nothing of Jesus.

Second, Daniel-Rops notes a few considerations which explain why even more was not written about Jesus in ancient times. For instance, the first century was certainly not characterized by advanced communications, at least by any recent standards. Any number of events, persons or situations could be newsworthy regionally and get hardly any attention on an international scene. Furthermore, there were very few ancient writers comparatively speaking. Consequently, they would have plenty to write about and often confined themselves to situations which were "official" or of international interest. At the outset we cannot be sure that Jesus or the earliest Christians made any such international commotion. Lastly, Jesus' background as a peasant from a humble family would mitigate any great amount of attention. Even the Christian teaching of his messiahship might look to an outsider as another Jewish "pretender" to be the king of the Jews.[61]

Again, we must not be misled by these considerations into the mistaken conclusion that extra-New Testament sources say nothing about

Jesus. There are a surprising number of non-Christian sources which do speak of him. There are also reasons why even more is not reported.

E. Summary and conclusion

We have investigated four misconceptions concerning the historicity of Jesus in this chapter, reaching the conclusion that none of them present compelling reasons to disregard all or part of our source material about him.

The charge that Jesus did not (or probably did not) exist is certainly a minority view and it emerges only infrequently. Its radical nature leaves it open to several especially strong negative critiques. It cannot stand in light of the early and eyewitness testimony presented by Paul and others, the early date, historicity and trustworthiness of the Gospels (as well as the New Testament as a whole) and the failure of legendary and mythical theories, such as the mystery religions, to explain Christian origins.

A more popular view asserts that Jesus did indeed exist but that very little can be known about him. But such efforts are also disproven by the data. The incorrect *a priori* dismissal of the possibility of miraculous events such as Jesus' resurrection, the absence of the required basis for early belief in the historical Jesus, the historical objections to radical form and redaction criticism and the demonstrated reliability of the New Testament text invalidate this second option.

Many prefer a more historical view which constructs a life of Jesus from the available records, apart from either doctrine or miracles. However, this view, while seemingly more compelling, also fails both by ruling out miracles *a priori*, and by its frequent denial of a historical investigation of miracle-claims. Also, such an approach fails in its naturalistic theorizing concerning the resurrection, as is even admitted by critics, and by ignoring the possibility that theology would very possibly be relevant if it could be shown that Jesus was literally raised from the dead in space-time history.

Lastly, some charge Christianity with having no extra-biblical references for Jesus' life at all. Not only is such a claim false, as will be shown in Part Two, but there are good reasons why there are not even more secular sources for the life of Jesus than the surprising number of ancient non-Christian sources which are available.

These four approaches to the historical Jesus therefore present no roadblock to our investigation of his life. Applying normal historical methodology to ancient non-Christian and Christian (non-New Testament) sources, early Christian creeds and archaeological evidence, we will examine what history tells us about the life of Jesus. But first we will study some more or less popularized presentations of Jesus which portray atypical views of his life.

Notes

[1]G. A. Wells' thesis is set forth in his works such as *Did Jesus Exist?* (Buffalo: Prometheus Books, 1975); "Was Jesus Crucified Under Pilate? Did He Even Exist at All?," *The Humanist*, volume XXXVIII, no. 1, January-February, 1978, pp. 22-27.

[2]See Wells' discussion of the Gospels in *Did Jesus Exist?* Cf. also "Was Jesus Crucified Under Pilate?" pp. 24, 26.

[3]Wells, "Was Jesus Crucified Under Pilate," pp. 24, 26.

[4]Ibid., p. 24.

[5]Ibid.; cf. *Did Jesus Exist?*, Chapter 5.

[6]For one such list, see Amedee Brunot, "The Gospel Before the Gospels" in *The Sources for the Life of Christ*, ed. by Henri Daniel-Rops (New York: Hawthorn Books, Inc., 1962), pp. 110-114; cf. also pp. 114f.

[7]For examples of the views of well-known critical scholars, see Daniel-Rops, Chapter IV, ibid., especially pp. 41-42, 50-85 and standard works such as Robert M. Grant, *An Historical Introduction to the New Testament* (London: Collins, 1963), Chapters VIII-XI in particular and Archibald Hunter, *Introducing the New Testament* second edition (Philadelphia: Westminster Press, 1957), especially pp. 41-63.

[8]Grant, *Jesus: An Historian's Review of the Gospels*, pp. 183-189.

[9]See Daniel-Rops, Robert M. Grant and Hunter.

[10]Michael Grant, pp. 199-200.

[11]Wolfhart Pannenberg, *Jesus-God and Man*, transl. by Lewis L. Wilkens and Duane A. Priebe (Philadelphia: The Westminster Press, 1968), p. 91.

[12]Cf. Wells, "Was Jesus Crucified Under Pilate?", p. 24, with Bruce M. Metzger, *Historical and Literary Studies: Pagan, Jewish and Christian* (Grand Rapids: William B. Eerdmans Publishing Co., 1968), especially pp. 18-19.

[13]Otto Pfleiderer, *The Early Christian Conception of Christ: Its Significance and Value in the History of Religion* (London: Williams and Norgate, 1905), pp. 153-154, 159.

[14]Metzger, pp. 11, 20-22; cf. Edwin Yamauchi, "Easter—Myth, Hallucination or History?" in *Christianity Today*, volume XVIII, no. 12, March 15, 1974, pp. 4-

7 and volume XVIII, no. 13, March 29, 1974, pp. 12-16.

[15]Michael Grant, p. 199.

[16]For examples, see Pannenberg, p. 91 and Metzger, p. 7.

[17]Rudolf Bultmann, "The Study of the Synoptic Gospels," in *Form Criticism*, transl. by Frederick C. Grant (New York: Harper and Brothers, 1962), p. 60.

[18]Rudolf Bultmann, *Jesus Christ and Mythology* (New York: Charles Scribner's Sons, 1958), pp. 16-20; cf. pp. 35-38.

[19]Rudolf Bultmann, "New Testament and Mythology" in *Kerygma and Myth*, ed. by Hans Werner Bartsch (New York: Harper and Row, Publishers, 1961), p. 38.

[20]Ibid., p. 42. Bultmann expresses the same view in his *Theology of the New Testament*, transl. by Kendrick Grobel, 2 vols. (New York: Charles Scribner's Sons, 1951, 1955), vol. I, p. 45.

[21]Bultmann, "The Study of the Synoptic Gospels," pp. 60-61, 64, 72.

[22]Rudolf Bultmann, *Jesus and the Word*, transl. by Louise Pettibone Smith and Erminie Huntress (New York: Charles Scribner's Sons, 1934), p. 8.

[23]Bultmann, *Theology of the New Testament*, vol. I, Chapter I in particular.

[24]John Macquarrie, *An Existentialist Theology: A Comparison of Heidegger and Bultmann* (New York: Harper and Row, Publishers, 1965), pp. 185-186.

[25]Ibid., p. 186.

[26]For some instances, see Luke 1:1-4; John 1:14; 20:30-31; Acts 2:22-38; 17:30-31; Heb. 2:3-4; II Pet. 1:16-18; I John 1:1-3.

[27]Macquarrie, p. 23.

[28]For an excellent treatment of this issue, see Carl F. H. Henry, *Frontiers in Modern Theology* (Chicago: Moody Press, 1965), pp. 15-24.

[29]Ibid., pp. 21-22 for an interview with Bultmann where he lists some of these facts.

[30]A. N. Sherwin-White, *Roman Society and Roman Law in the New Testament* (London: Oxford University Press, 1963), p. 187.

[31]Michael Grant, *Jesus*, especially pp. 175-184; 198-201.

[32]Ibid., p. 182.

[33]Sherwin-White, p. 189.

[34]Ibid., p. 187.

[35]For more complete data concerning these points of critique, see Sherwin-White, ibid., pp. 186-193 and Grant, especially pp. 180-184.

[36]Grant, pp. 199-200; Sherwin-White, pp. 186-187.

[37]See F. F. Bruce, *The New Testament Documents: Are They Reliable?* (Grand Rapids: William B. Eerdmans Publishing Company, 1967), especially p. 16; John A. T. Robinson, *Can We Trust the New Testament?* (Grand Rapids: William B. Eerdmans Publishing Company, 1977), especially p. 36.

[38]Bruce, pp. 16-18; Robinson, pp. 36-37; Daniel-Rops, pp. 41-42.

[39]Bruce, p. 16; Robinson, pp. 37-38.

[40]Macquarrie, p. 168; Gordon H. Clark, "Bultmann's Three-Storied Universe" in *Christianity Today*, ed. by Frank Gaebelein (Westwood: Fleming H. Revell Company, 1966), pp. 218-219.

[41]Carl F. H. Henry, "Cross-Currents in Contemporary Theology", in *Jesus of Nazareth: Saviour and Lord*, ed. by Carl F. H. Henry (Grand Rapids: William B. Eerdmans Publishing Company, 1966), p. 15; Clark, pp. 217-218.

[42]Avery Dulles, "Jesus of History and Christ of Faith" in *Commonweal*, Nov. 24, 1967, pp. 225-232.

[43]Schubert Ogden, *Christ Without Myth* (New York: Harper and Row, Publishers, 1961).

[44]Michael Grant, *Jesus*, p. 13.

[45]Ibid., see pp. 180-182, 199-200, for instance.

[46]James M. Robinson, *A New Quest of the Historical Jesus* (London: SCM Press LTD, 1959), pp. 37-38.

[47]For the classic investigation of such old liberal attempts, see Albert Schweitzer, *The Quest of the Historical Jesus*, transl. by W. Montgomery from the 1906 German edition (New York: The Macmillan Company, 1968), pp. 3-4.

[48]Ibid., pp. 49-55.

[49]For example, see Habermas, "Skepticism: Hume," pp. 23-49.

[50]William Wand, pp. 70-71.

[51](Grand Rapids: Baker Book House, 1980).

[52]Maier, pp. 105-122; Yamauchi, March 15, 1974, pp. 4-7 and March 29, 1974, pp. 12-16; Wand, pp. 29-31, 51-52, 93-94; Montgomery, pp. 70-73, 93.

[53]Schweitzer, p. 56.

[54]See the excellent 1908 work by James Orr, *The Resurrection of Jesus* (Grand Rapids: Zondervan Publishing House, 1965). Cf. Gary Habermas, *The Resurrection of Jesus: A Rational Inquiry* (Ann Arbor: University Microfilms, 1976), especially pp. 114-171.

[55]Karl Barth, *The Doctrine of Reconciliation*, vol. IV of *Church Dogmatics*, transl. by G. W. Bromily and T. F. Torrance (Edinburgh: T. and T. Clark, 1956), p. 340.

[56]Raymond E. Brown, "The Resurrection and Biblical Criticism," in *Commonweal*, November 24, 1967, p. 233.

[57]See Habermas, *The Resurrection of Jesus: A Rational Inquiry*, pp. 191-193.

[58]The chain of argument is long, but the interested reader is referred to Habermas, *The Resurrection of Jesus: An Apologetic*.

[59]Shepard Clough, Nina Garsoian and David L. Hicks, *Ancient and Medieval*, vol. I of *A History of the Western World*, 3 vols. (Boston: D. C. Heath and Company, 1964) p. 127.

[60]Charles Templeton, *Act of God* (New York: Bantam Books, 1979), p. 152.

[61]Daniel-Rops, "The Silence of Jesus' Contemporaries," pp. 13-14, 17-18.

3

Popularistic Lives of Jesus

In addition to the major historical approaches to the life of Jesus presented in the last chapter, many have attempted to write more or less popularistic lives of Jesus. These often advocate unorthodox interpretations such as Jesus never dying on the cross, or his connections with the Qumran community, or his gnostic tendencies, or his trips to various parts of the world during the so-called "silent years," or trips even after the crucifixion. While such works are usually rejected by careful scholars, these attempts are sometimes very popular with lay people who are not familiar with the facts behind such questions. Herein lies the major reason that these approaches are included in this book. Many people are disturbed by illogical or nonfactual presentations, but are not quite able to locate the problems involved.

First, our procedure will be to take a general look at similar popularistic lives of Jesus which were written 100-150 years ago in order to ascertain their fate. Then we will investigate several of the most popular recent attempts to present unorthodox pictures of Jesus' life.

A. The fictitious lives of Jesus

From the late eighteenth through the nineteenth centuries there were various attempts to formulate what Schweitzer called the "fictitious lives of Jesus." He remarked that they were chiefly characterized as the works of "a few imperfectly equipped free-lances."[1]

These works often attempted to invent the inner motivations of Jesus' life which are not reported in the Gospels. Usually a secret organization or association was postulated. This was often the Essenes, who were portrayed as leading but secret members of society, who manipulated events and circumstances in Jesus' life. Schweitzer refers to these "plots" as "rather a sorry makeshift."[2]

Karl Bahrdt wrote one of the first such works, a multi-volumed effort, between 1784 and 1792. For Bahrdt, Nicodemus and Joseph of Arimathea were Essenes who endeavored to keep their identity a secret. Jesus became involved with this secret order at an early age and later became a valued member. Through the efforts and management of this private group, Jesus staged "miracles" during his ministry. Luke, in particular, was responsible for the healing miracles. The Essenes were also responsible for plotting Jesus' death, whereby Luke was able to administer drugs and also cause Jesus to resist death. After surviving crucifixion he was nursed back to health, which enabled him to visit with his followers on several occasions.[3]

Perhaps the best known and most emulated of the fictitious lives was one written by Karl Venturini between 1800 and 1802. Again, Jesus was protected and trained from his youth by the Essenes. During his public ministry, his "miracles" were not supernatural but his healings were performed by the use of medicines. While Venturini did not propose a plot in Jesus' death, Joseph of Arimathea and Nicodemus noticed signs that Jesus might still be alive while they were preparing his body for burial and they signaled the Essenes, who later removed his body from the tomb. After having recovered somewhat, Jesus made periodic visits to his disciples.[4]

Later, fictitious lives by writers such as Gfrörer (written between 1831 and 1838), Hennell (1839) and Salvator (1838) all postulated that the Essenes were involved in many aspects of Jesus' ministry. All three authors likewise asserted that Jesus was nursed back to health by the Essenes after his crucifixion so that he could visit his followers.[5]

Through such works we supposedly perceive some of the inner workings of Jesus' life and ministry, which is inextricably intertwined with the Essenes. In every case presented here, Jesus is spared death, is nursed back to health by this secret group and recovers sufficiently to visit with his disciples.

Such attempts to construct a speculative life of Jesus have not attracted much scholarly attention. They were plainly based on supposition and thus could add little to historical studies of Jesus' life. But, as we will perceive, some modern popularistic lives of Jesus are quite similar to these fictitious works of about 150 years ago.

B. The swoon theory

All five of the fictitous lives of Jesus just discussed taught that Jesus survived death on the cross and, instead, was revived. His "appearances" to his disciples, of course, were not miraculous, for he had never died. The swoon theory, also espoused by Paulus, was quite popular in the first half of the nineteenth century. As discussed in Chapter II, it was one of the naturalistic theories against the resurrection. It was disproven by the facts and indicted by the liberal scholarship. Before examining this view, it will be helpful to present an overview of two contemporary attempts to write similar lives of Jesus.

Hugh Schonfield's *The Passover Plot* created quite a sensation when it appeared.[6] However, very few readers were aware of the similarity between this book and earlier fictitious lives of Jesus. For Schonfield, Jesus had carefully planned his career of public ministry in accordance with his belief that he was Israel's Messiah.[7] Accordingly, he plotted events such as his triumphal entry into Jerusalem, on which occasion Lazarus helped him make the appropriate arrangements.[8] Jesus made especially intricate plans concerning his upcoming crucifixion, which required especially accurate timing. On this occasion his chief confident was Joseph of Arimathea.[9]

While Jesus was on the cross, Joseph made arrangements for an unidentified man to give Jesus a drink that had been drugged. As a result, Jesus slipped quickly into a state of unconsciousness, which made him appear dead. Nonetheless, Jesus was in a very serious condition when he was removed from the cross, especially complicated by John's report of the spear wound in his chest.[10] On Saturday, Jesus' body was removed from the tomb, after which he regained consciousness briefly, but died shortly thereafter and was reburied.[11]

At this point, Schonfield turns to his proposed reconstruction of events that account for the disciples' belief in Jesus' resurrection. The unidentified man at the cross who administered the drug is the key figure in this reconstruction. He helped carry Jesus to the tomb, then returned on Saturday to rescue him. During Jesus' brief period of consciousness, Jesus asked this man to convey to his disciples that he had risen from the dead. However, Jesus died shortly after and this person helped bury him. It is also this anonymous person who was present in the tomb when the women came early on Sunday morning and was the one mistaken by Mary Magdalene as the gardener. Later this same man visited the disciples on the road to Emmaus, at the seashore and in Galilee. The disciples mistook this stranger for Jesus and proclaimed his resurrection from the dead.[12]

It should be obvious to the reasonably impartial reader that this incredible sequence of events, where an unidentified man simply "appears" very conveniently whenever there is a need to explain anything away, is extremely questionable, to say the least. The entire plot closely parallels the fictitious lives of Jesus which are now so outdated and ignored by serious scholars. Indeed, even Schonfield admits that much of his account "is an imaginative reconstruction."[13] Later he explains that "We are nowhere claiming for our reconstruction that it represents what actually happened."[14] According to John A. T. Robinson, *The Passover Plot* is an example of a popularistic book which is factually groundless enough that, if the public was not so interested in virtually anyone who writes on Christianity, it "would be laughed out of court."[15] Therefore, we assert that there is a very high improbability against Schonfield's reconstruction of Jesus' life.

One other example of the swoon theory in popular literature is Donovan Joyce's *The Jesus Scroll*.[16] The thesis of this book, which contains an even more incredible string of improbabilities than Schonfield's, will be left for a later section of this chapter. However, Joyce's account of the swoon theory is discussed here.

For Joyce, Jesus was also planning his escape from death on the cross. Accordingly, he was drugged and the Roman soldiers did not examine Jesus too closely, perhaps because they had been bribed. Neither did they stab him in the side with a spear in order to insure his death. As a result, Jesus did not die on the cross. Rather, he was resuscitated in the tomb, apparently by a doctor who had been concealed inside ahead of time.[17]

This account of Jesus' swoon likewise smacks of fictitious aspects, similar to both Schonfield and the eighteenth and nineteenth century attempts.

C. The swoon theory refuted

The swoon theory was perhaps the most popular naturalistic theory against the historicity of Jesus' resurrection in the early nineteenth century. But David Strauss, himself a liberal theologian, disproved this theory to the satisfaction of his fellow scholars.

Strauss raised a very important issue. Even if it was imagined that Jesus was able to survive Roman crucifixion, what could he do about the heavy stone in the entrance to the tomb? In his extremely weakened physical condition, could he move an object which even a healthy man would have a great problem with (according to tradition)? This would be even more difficult when it is remembered that the stone would have to be rolled uphill out of its gulley. Additionally, the inside of the stone would provide no edge against which Jesus might at least use his weight to push. Then, even if he could have escaped from the tomb, could he walk the distance to the disciples' hiding place after having his weight suspended on a Roman crucifixion spike just a short time previous?

Yet, Strauss' most convincing point concerned Jesus' condition upon reaching his disciples. Very few would doubt that he would be in sad physical shape, limping badly, bleeding, pale and clutching his side. He would obviously be in need of physical assistance and, at any rate, would not appear to be the resurrected and glorified Lord of Life! As Strauss pointed out, the disciples would have gone for a doctor's help rather than proclaim Jesus the risen Son of God! Strauss asserted that even if the swoon theory was conceivable, it still could not account for the disciples' belief in the risen Jesus. Since they did proclaim him to be resurrected and glorified Lord, the swoon theory is not able to account for the facts.[18]

Shortly after the turn of the century, Schweitzer referred to Strauss' critique as the "death-blow" to such rationalistic approaches.[19] After Strauss' views were circulated, the liberal "lives of Jesus" usually shunned the swoon theory.[20] By the early twentieth century, other critical scholars proclaimed this theory to be nothing more than a historical curiousity of the past. Even critics no longer considered it to be a viable hypothesis.[21]

Modern research has levelled at least three additional critiques against the swoon theory. First, crucifixion is essentially death by asphyxiation, as the intercostal and pectoral muscles around the lungs halt normal breathing while the body hangs in the "down" position. Therefore, faking death on the cross still would not permit one to breathe; one cannot fake the inability to breathe for any length of time. Breaking the victim's ankles insured death even quicker, since the person could not push up in order to free the lungs for breathing. The Romans were knowledgeable in these matters, as indicated by the broken leg bones of a first century crucifixion victim whose skeleton was recently discovered (see Chapter VII for details). Since Jesus' ankles were not broken, we have the Roman's assurance that he was previously dead. Otherwise, this method would have killed him. Either way, the end result of Jesus' death is very probable.

Second, an even stronger refutation of the swoon theory is gained from the medical conclusion that the Roman lance entered Jesus' heart. The gospel writer probably never understood the medical significance of what he recorded, for which eyewitness testimony is claimed (John 19:34-35). Medical doctors who have studied this issue usually agree that this is a very accurate medical description. The water probably proceeded from the pericardium, the sac that surrounds the heart, while the blood came from the right side of the heart. Even if Jesus was alive before he was stabbed, the lance would almost certainly have killed him.[22] Therefore, this chest wound also disproves the swoon theory.

Third, if the Shroud of Turin is the authentic burial garment of Jesus (see Chapter VII), it would provide one final criticism of this theory, for the man buried in this cloth is dead, as indicated by the evidence.

The physical condition of Jesus, as advocated by Strauss, the nature of death on the cross by asphyxiation, the study of the chest wound and the Shroud of Turin combine to entirely abrogate the swoon theory. Additionally, we witnessed the difficulties above (with Schonfield and Joyce) in the actual implementation of this view. Therefore, it is no surprise that this hypothesis is rejected today by critics.[23]

D. Qumran connections

Another popularistic picture of Jesus is that he was a member of the Essene Community at Qumran, which is said to have influenced his teachings tremendously. Sometimes, but seldom, he is even connected with the Essene "Teacher of Righteousness," a priest who called the people to obey the Law and to live a holy life before the Lord and was perhaps even martyred for his teachings.

For instance, Upton Ewing's *The Essene Christ* asserts that Jesus was raised as an Essene and belonged to the sect, as did John the Baptist.[24] It is even hinted that Jesus thought of himself as the "Teacher of Righteousness."[25] Because of this background of both John and Jesus, their followers were likewise influenced by Essene teachings. Subsequently, the four Gospels are said to have borrowed much from the Qumran community.[26]

Strangely enough, Ewing sees the major theme of the Essene community, including Jesus and the early Christians, as the teaching of monistic ethics. This teaching involves a type of pantheistic oneness of the entire universe with God, each other and all of life. As a result, no violence should be perpetrated on any creature or person, but we should live in peace and love with all.[27]

Another writer to link Jesus and Christian origins with the Qumran community is Charles Potter. He also suggests that both John the Baptist and Jesus studied at Qumran while growing up. This would explain where Jesus was during his so-called "silent years" between the ages of twelve and thirty.[28] During these years, Potter postulates that Jesus either wrote, or at least read and was very influenced by an apocalyptic book named *The Secrets of Enoch*, which is closely connected with the ideas taught by the Essenes. While, at the very least, Jesus was inspired by these teachings, Potter is careful to point out that Jesus was not the Essene "Teacher of Righteousness," who lived long before Jesus.[29]

These works of Ewing and Potter are examples of popularistic attempts to explain the inner motivations and secret events of Jesus' life that are not recorded in the New Testament. Like the fictitious lives of Jesus described by Schweitzer, not only do we find an interest in these inner workings, we also confront the secretive organization of the Essenes once again. And like Schweitzer's examples, so are these works refuted by the facts. Four critiques of these views are now presented.

First, there is a train of illogic employed in these works. For Ewing, the connection between Jesus and the Essenes is based on the opinion that, since he was neither a Sadducee nor a Pharisee, Jesus must have been an Essene![30] Again, since the Gospels depict Jesus as opposing both the Sadducees and the Pharisees but never opposing the Essenes, then he must have been one of the latter.[31]

Both of these statements are textbook examples of arguments from silence. Just because there is an absence of evidence in the Gospels as to what group Jesus favored, we cannot argue from that silence to the fact that he favored the Essenes. For instance, the Talmud fails to mention the Essenes, so does this make it an Essene book? These statements also commit the black-white fallacy of logic. They assume that either Jesus had to be a Sadducee or Pharisee on the one hand or an Essene on the other. But this conclusion only follows if it is known that these are the only options. Jesus could have been a member of another group or of no group at all. Indeed, the Gospels depict him as one who was "his own man" without explicit support for any sectarian politics.

Potter argues similarly. He states that he applied the logic which he learned in college to the facts concerning *The Secrets of Enoch* and decided that there was "no convincing reason against Jesus' authorship."[32]

With this logic he surely should have noticed that his argument was also from silence. An absence of reasons against Jesus' authorship provides no evidence that he did, in fact, write the book. Potter additionally argues that *The Secrets of Enoch* was written by one author, from 1-50 A.D.[33] This is also an argument from the absence of evidence. There were surely an enormous number of intelligent people who lived between these years who would, given accurate dates, also be candidates for authorship. But this is not evidence that Jesus was the author. In concession, Potter even admits that his thesis is somewhat "imaginative."[34]

The second major reason for rejecting this thesis is that, while there are similarities between Jesus and Qumran,[35] there are also many differences which oppose any close connection. As asserted by Brownlee, "The Qumran literature tells us much about the background of primitive Christianity, but it can tell us nothing directly about Jesus.[36] A number of scholars have noted several differences between Jesus and Qumran beliefs.[37] (1) Jesus opposed legalism, whereas the Essenes held strictly to it. (2) Jesus also opposed ceremonial purity, while the Essenes, again, adherred strictly to it. (3) The Essenes taught that even the Messiah would be purified from sin by suffering, while this opposes Christian teachings of the sinlessness of Jesus. (4) The Qumran community was looking for two (or even three) messiahs, while Jesus was both already present and had all messianic aspects combined in himself.

(5) The Essenes give little or no place to the concept of the Kingdom of God, while this is Jesus' central teaching. (6) "Love," as the major Christian ethic, does not appear in Essene teachings. (7) Jesus' ethics are judged to be closer to Rabbinic literature than to Qumran. (8) Jesus taught that salvation would also be extended to the Gentiles while the Essenes were more exclusivistic. (9) According to Josephus, the Essenes taught the immortality of the soul, which is contrasted with the Christian teaching of the resurrection of the body.

As a result, it is generally held that a close connection between Jesus and Qumran is very improbable.[38] Daniélou even states:

> Must we then conclude that he was an Essene, at least at some period of his life? Here historians are unanimous in affirming the contrary. There is nothing either in his origins or in the setting in which he habitually lived, to justify such a conclusion.[39]

Our third critique opposes the minority opinion that Jesus was the Essenes' "Teacher of Righteousness." Although very few hold this view, we will still list several problems noted by scholars.[40] (1) The Essenes' Teacher was a priest, as opposed to Jesus' plural office. (2) The Teacher considered himself a sinner in need of purification, while Jesus was sinless. (3) The Teacher perceived that he was separated by an infinite gulf from God, while Christians hold that Jesus is the very Son of God.

(4) There is no evidence of any atoning value being placed on the Teacher's death, while such is the special significance of Jesus' shed blood and death. (5) There is no claim or evidence that the Teacher was raised from the dead, while this is the central event for Christianity. (6) Jesus is worshipped by Christians as God, while such was not the practice of the Essenes and even opposed their belief. (7) Additionally, the Essenes' Teacher lived long before Jesus did.

Our fourth critique of this view is the strongest. While the point is often missed, this view is not necessarily critical of Christ or his teachings even if it was shown that he had affinities to Essene thought or even that he was a member of the group. As Pfeiffer explains:

> It should be observed that there is nothing derogatory to the person of Christ in the assumption that He or His followers were of Essene background. The Scriptures make it clear that the mother of our Lord was a Jewess, and that He became incarnate in the midst of a Jewish environment. If it were proved that this environment was also Essene, Christian theology would lose nothing and the uniqueness of Jesus would be no more disproved than it is disproved by the assertion of the Jewish origin after the flesh.[41]

In other words, Jesus had to be born somewhere and he went to school somewhere. To assert that this background was influenced by the Essenes is not in itself critical of Christianity, as long as his teachings are not adjusted or his uniqueness modified. His person and teachings are still validated by a trustworthy New Testament (see Chapter II) and, if his resurrection is verified, this could also serve to confirm his message.[42]

Yet, we must still reject this approach to the life of Jesus. The illogical argumentation, the differences between Christianity and Qumran and the differences between Jesus and the Teacher of Righteousness all invalidate it. However, even if this hypothesis was demonstrated, it would affect nothing of major importance in Christianity since Jesus did have some type of background and his message can be shown to be trustworthy and unique anyway.

E. Gnostic influences

A recurring topic in treatments of Jesus and Christian origins concerns the influence of gnosticism, an early hellenistic philosophy which stressed such themes as a God who did not create matter, a body/soul dualism, the quest for salvation through special knowledge (*gnosis*) and immortality of the soul. According to recent scholarship, some of the earliest gnostic gospels could be dated from 150-200 A.D., while most of the gnostic treatises are later.[43]

Those who pursue these theses of gnostic influence present some differences of interpretation, however. According to Elaine Pagels' hypothesis, there were wide ranges of variations of doctrine and belief in the early church. In her opinion, the New Testament canon was not settled until the late second century A.D. As a result, the canonical Gospels were widely circulated along with other gospels, such as those composed by the gnostics.[44]

One question by Pagels concerns whether the canonical Gospels have a greater claim to authenticity, especially when some of Jesus' words might be interpreted in a gnostic context.[45] At any rate, there is no question that interpretations varied greatly between orthodox believers and the gnostics.[46] Nonetheless, the orthodox Christians achieved "victory" over the gnostics in issues of theology and interpretation by the end of the third century. Yet this does not mean that the gnostics did not have greater insight into the original teachings of Christianity. As such, gnosticism remains a possible alternative to orthodoxy.[47]

Another approach is taken by A. Powell Davies, who postulates that the teachings of Christianity, gnosticism and the Essenes were all current at the same time and exerted influence on each other. In this intense struggle over important theological issues, the Christians were victorious in the second and third centuries A.D.[48] However, Christianity emerged from this struggle after having its theology affected by the gnostics and the Essenes. Early in its infancy, Christianity was very much an offshoot of Judaism. But Paul had taken the message to the Gentiles, an act not anticipated by Jesus. Through its growth, however, Christianity was no longer a Jewish message about the Kingdom of God but gradually became a syncretistic collection of many religions.[49]

By such approaches we are chiefly concerned with the confrontation between Christian orthodoxy and gnosticism. Both Pagels and Davies raise the question concerning the authentic origins of Christianity. Can we be sure that the New Testament canon (and the Gospels in particular) does preserve the essence of Jesus' teachings? Their hypotheses that gnosticism is perhaps a valid alternative to orthodoxy (Pagels) or that Christianity gradually (by the third century A.D.) became a syncretistic faith incorporating the beliefs of many systems (Davies) are both inadequate answers, as revealed in the four following critiques. Additional comments from the next section of this chapter will also apply to Davies' view.

First, the four canonical Gospels are much earlier than the gnostic gospels and were established much better with regard to their authority in the early church. Again, while the earliest gnostic gospels are dated from about 150-200 A.D. (as pointed out in Chapter I), the canonical Gospels are dated from 65-100 A.D., which is approximately one century earlier on the average. Even though these gnostic sources possibly include earlier material, the Gospels certainly include traditions which are much earlier.

Thus, while Pagels would have us think that all of the canonical and non-canonical gospels circulated together for people to judge in spite of the differences in age,[50] the facts indicate that these groups of sources were not on equal footing. The very fact that the canonical Gospels were about 100 years older is a preliminary indication that they could possibly be closer to the events in question.

Second, the evidence strongly indicates that the New Testament (and the Gospels in particular) was under the control of eyewitness testimony. Pagels realizes the importance of this point as well.[51] In Chapter II we already discussed the early and eyewitness testimony to Jesus' resurrection as recorded in 1 Cor. 15:3ff., a point which critics fully admit. But there are many recognized critical scholars who accept eyewitness testimony behind the Gospels as well.[52] For instance, the author of the second gospel is usually asserted to be John Mark, who is believed to have recorded the testimony of Peter, an apostle and eyewitness.[53] Matthew is taken even by critical scholars to be the author of the Q document (a major source, *Quelle*, behind the first gospel) and thereby provides eyewitness testimony.[54] It is usually held that Luke is the author of both the third gospel and the book of Acts, which provides further firsthand testimony since Luke collected his information from eyewitnesses (Luke 1:1-4).[55] Part of the reason for the growing interest in the fourth gospel is that it is often linked closely with the eyewitness testimony of the apostle John as its major source.[56]

Coming from critical theologians, these convictions concerning the eyewitness and even apostolic testimony behind the Gospels and Acts are very probable indications of the trustworthiness of the information concerning Jesus Christ. As A. M. Hunter asserts, the Gospels are trustworthy for several reasons. (1) The earliest Christians were very careful to preserve the tradition of Jesus' life and teachings. (2) The gospel authors were close to the eyewitnesses and thus had access to the facts about Jesus. (3) The gospel writers were apparently honest reporters. (4) The picture of Jesus as presented in the four Gospels is virtually the same.[57] Far from not knowing which of the canonical or the gnostic teachings concerning Jesus are historical, the evidence is quite strong in favor of the New Testament Gospels.

In our third critique of this gnostic thesis we note that Jesus' teachings in the Gospels are interpreted in a variety of ways, but this is much different from asserting that his statements support gnosticism. While there are teachings about light and darkness, found in John, and occasionally in the synoptics, this dualism is considered very Palestinian and not gnostic. This conclusion was one of the major results obtained from the studies of the Dead Sea Scrolls.[58]

However, Jesus' teachings in the Gospels do not conform to the major tenets of gnosticism. For instance, Jesus does not refer to Yahweh as less than the supreme Creator and God of the universe. Neither does he speak of the physical body as a necessary evil which imprisons the soul. With regard to eternal life, Jesus taught the resurrection of the body, not the immortality of the soul. And when Jesus taught his disciples truth which he did not share with the crowds, this had no affinity to the special *gnosis* of the gnostics, for Jesus taught his disciples to share his words with the world (Matt. 28:19-20; Luke 24:47, 48; Acts 1:8). Additionally, salvation, which is available to all, is through faith in the death and resurrection of Jesus as payment for personal sin, not through secret types of mystical knowledge.

Pagels notes other differences between the teachings of Jesus and those of the gnostics, such as his blessings on marriage and his stress on its nearly inviolable status, his interest in children and his compassion for physical suffering.[59] Thus those who would champion the cause of early gnosticism reach this third obstacle, in that Jesus' gospel teachings do not readily lend themselves to any gnostic reinterpretation.

The fourth problem with this thesis is the contention that the New Testament canon was in flux until the late second century, allowing a variety of gospels to circulate without any indication as to which ones were authoritative.[60] Such an assessment is not in keeping with the facts. Within the pages of the New Testament itself the canon was already beginning to form. In 1 Tim. 5:18 two references are called "Scripture." The first one is found in Deut. 25:4, one of the most sacred books of the Law. The second quotation is taken from Luke 10:7 (compare Matt. 10:10), which records the words of Jesus. By placing verses in Deuteronomy and Luke (plus Matthew) together as Scripture, we have an indication of the early acceptance of the canonical Gospels as accurate treatises concerning Jesus' teaching. While it does not directly concern the Gospels, we might also point out that 2 Pet. 3:15-16 lists Paul's epistles as Scripture.

So very early, even before the last canonical book was written, two collections of books were already being referred to as Scripture. These were the Gospels (including Acts) and Paul's epistles. Such conclusions concerning these two collections are supported by a number of other very early sources as well.[61] In his epistle to the *Corinthians*, dated about 95 A.D., Clement of Rome made an important reference to the "Gospel," which was the message that the apostles had received from Christ and had passed on to the church (42). Identifying the nature of the material to which he was referring, Clement cited portions found in Matthew, Mark and Luke, introducing them as the words of Jesus (13, 46). Here we have an early, first century reference to this collection of canonical Gospels, which were recognized as the words of Jesus. Clement even thought of them as a unit, using the singular "Gospel" to describe their combined testimony, as did the other early commentators.

Ignatius, writing seven epistles ca. 110-115 A.D. on his way to Rome to suffer martyrdom, quoted Luke 24:39 as the words of Jesus (Smyrnaeans 3). Polycarp wrote his "Epistle to the Philippians" ca. 115 A.D., shortly after Ignatius' letters and at least partially to inquire as to the fate of Ignatius (13). Polycarp also quotes portions found in all three synoptic Gospels and, again, refers to them as the words of the Lord (2, 7). Again we see canonical Gospels taken as the source for Jesus' words.

The "Didache," an ancient manual of Christianity, is usually dated somewhere between the end of the first century and the early second century A.D. It refers twice to the "Gospel" which contains the words of Jesus and, in both instances, immediately cites portions found in all three synoptic Gospels (8, 15-16).

The epistle of *Barnabas*, dated about 135 A.D., refers to Matt. 22:14 as

"Scripture" (4). It then speaks of the apostles' "Gospel," which is followed with a quote from the synoptics (Matt. 9:13; Mark 2:17; Luke 5:32) as the message of Jesus (5).

From Papias' *Exposition of Oracles of the Lord* we obtain information on the writing of the Gospels, found in the fragments which are all that remain of this work. Papias explains that Mark wrote his gospel, based on the teaching of Peter, while Matthew wrote his account in Hebrew, with interested readers composing their own translations (III). Concerning John, Papias relates that he composed his gospel while he was an elderly man (XIX, XX). Papias also cites the text of John 8:1-11 as the words of Jesus (IV). Incidently, a number of traditions state that Papias was a student of the apostle John and even penned the last gospel as John dictated it to him.[62]

Therefore, the facts certainly indicate that the New Testament Gospels were accepted as canonical well before the late second century. Not only are they approved, in principle, in 1 Tim. 5:18, where Luke is specifically called Scripture, but six major Christian sources refer to them as the gospel, the words of Christ and Scripture between 95 and 140 A.D.

While the Gospels were one major collection of books in the New Testament canon which were received as soon as they were written, the other was Paul's epistles. Besides being called Scripture in 2 Pet. 3:15-16, verses from Paul's epistles are referred to as inspired in Clement's *Corinthians* (47), Ignatius' *Ephesians* (10) and in his letter *To Polycarp* (5) as well as in Polycarp's *Philippians* (1, 3-4, 6). In this latter source Paul's letters as a whole are referred to as Scripture (11-12). Davies' thesis that Paul perverted Jesus' message is also rejected by the earliest sources, which view Paul's epistles as teaching the same message as the Gospels.

At any rate, when the earliest gnostic gospels were being written in the second half of the second century A.D., the canonical Gospels had already been well established as Scripture. In fact, the Nag Hammadi gnostic texts cite most of the canonical New Testament books and borrow from some of these books often. The *Gospel of Truth* and the *Gospel of Phillip*, in particular, recognize most of the New Testament as authoritative.[63] The canonical Gospels were therefore not "forced" into the New Testament, despite Pagels complaint that history is written by the victors.[64] The canonical Gospels were "victors" for a reason—the facts indicate that they are simply better attested sources for the teachings of Jesus. Even the gnostic texts themselves recognized this.

Our conclusion that the four canonical Gospels are better sources for the teachings of Jesus was based on several lines of evidence. They are both much earlier than their gnostic counterparts and they are based on eyewitness testimony, which cannot be said of the gnostic gospels. Additionally, Jesus was not a gnostic and neither do his teachings reflect that philosophy. Lastly, the canon was formulated much more quickly than is often assumed. The four Gospels, in particular, were recognized as the inspired teaching of Jesus shortly after they were written, as indicated by both early orthodox and later gnostic citings. Thus, the four canonical Gospels provide an early, eyewitness and trustworthy foundation for studying the life and teachings of Jesus.

F. Jesus' message is changed by others

The charge is often made that Jesus' message was actually quite different from the one which Christians have traditionally taught concerning him. This sometimes is said to be the case, for instance, because the Gospels represent the teachings of the early church and not those of Jesus himself, (compare the discussion about Bultmann above). We saw how this approach is invalidated as an attempt to ascertain Jesus' teachings. On the other hand, Davies' thesis, as just observed, claimed that Paul changed the direction of Christianity, and allowed the later syncretism of the third century, which was also shown to be in error.

Hugh Schonfield postulated another reason for this change in Jesus' message. He holds that Jesus was a teacher who was true to Judaism and who had no desire to start any new religion. That is why, for instance, he never proclaimed his own deity.[65] While Paul did present some different teachings,[66] he is not the real culprit. Rather, Schonfield asserts that the church at Rome perverted Paul's teachings about Jesus in order to turn him into a deity who set up a new religion.[67] The Roman church did this by consciously writing some of the New Testament books and by influencing others to rewrite the story of Jesus. Books said to be either written or influenced strongly by this effort include the synoptic Gospels, Hebrews and Peter's epistles.[68] The general movement is from Jesus' original teachings, to Paul's assessments, to the Roman redirection.[69] The result is that Christian theology as it is taught today is not the teachings of Jesus and the apostles.[70] By such progress, the teachings of Jesus and Paul have been changed by a plot to make Christianity palatable to Roman gentiles. In spite of Schonfield's new "twists," his thesis is vulnerable to four criticisms.

First, since Schonfield rejects the testimony of the Gospels,[71] he presents no valid basis on which to assert that Jesus' original teachings were different from what traditional Christianity believes about him. The problem here is actually twofold. Initially, Schonfield is opposed by all of the evidence for the authenticity and trustworthiness of the Gospels (and the New Testament). Additionally, and more specifically, how can one rule out the Gospel's testimony and still have a basis on which to assert that the original teachings of Jesus were different? How can Schonfield know that Jesus did not present the message of the Gospels? What is his basis of comparison between Jesus and what the earliest sources say about him? It becomes apparent that there are no grounds of distinction between Jesus and the Gospels.

Schonfield might respond that Jesus could not have taught the message that traditional Christianity affirms, since it was contrary to what first century Jews believed. Yet Schonfield uses the Gospels to establish this response,[72] a basis which he rejects. And since it is not a proper hermeneutical method to pick and choose the verses which one will accept and those which one will reject, he is again left without any valid basis for his position.

For those who contend that the Gospels are dependable sources which reveal a non-divine Jesus and that Paul (or others) perverted this message, it should be mentioned here that even the synoptic Gospels reveal that Jesus claimed deity for himself. For example, he referred to himself as "Son of God" and "Son of Man," he taught that salvation was found only in himself and claimed that only he had the power to forgive sin.[73] He certainly claimed to be in a privileged relationship with God; his usage of "Abba" (Aramaic for "Daddy") is a very unusual name for God and is an indication of his unique sonship, as many critical scholars admit.[74]

At any rate, we cannot follow Schonfield and attempt to divorce Jesus' message from what the earliest sources indicate concerning him, for in so doing we destroy the basis which is needed to establish that divison. Additionally, to assume that Jesus did not consider himself deity while ruling out the Gospels, is to do so on the grounds of the presumed first century Jewish thought, which is a circular argument that presupposes Jesus did not teach anything different. This is the very point to be demonstrated.

Second, there is no evidence for any such plot on the part of Christians at Rome, as presumed by Schonfield. Since we do not know that

Jesus denied deity and especially since there are reasons to assert that he did claim such deity then why would there be a need for Roman Christians to "invent" the message? In other words, we can only begin to contemplate the alteration of Jesus' words if we know that he did not teach the message of his deity in the first place. But since this point is invalid, as just shown, one cannot leap to the next step of a conspiracy by the Christians at Rome.

Third, the Pauline epistles, which even Schonfield accepts as valid texts, attest to the orthodox view of Jesus' deity. Thus, while Schonfield holds that Paul followed Jesus' own teachings in rejecting the deity of the Messiah,[75] the writings of Paul which are accepted by Schonfield teach otherwise. This is revealed even by a brief survey. In Rom. 1:3-4, Paul gives Jesus the titles "Son," "Lord" and "Christ." Although completely ignored by Schonfield in a treatment of this verse,[76] the usage of "Lord," in particular, indicates Paul's view of Jesus' deity. As said by Oscar Cullmann in his classic Christology, this term indicates that Paul could give Jesus the title of "God," since "Lord" itself "clearly expresses Jesus' deity."[77]

Even stronger is Paul's statement in Rom. 9:5, where Jesus is, in all probability, actually called "God."[78] Similarly, Paul affirms Christ's full deity in Col. 2:9. While Schonfield clearly mistranslates this latter verse,[79] Cullmann, agreeing with virtually all scholars, renders the key phrase as "the whole fullness of deity dwells bodily" in Jesus Christ.[80] As philologist A. T. Robinson points out, this verse indicates that all the fullness of the very essence of God dwells in Jesus in bodily form.[81] These two references, in particular, reveal Paul's view of the full deity of Jesus.

Other passages are additionally helpful. Philippians 2:6-11 asserts that Jesus has the form or very nature of God and commends worship of the exalted Jesus. In Col. 1:15, Paul points out that Jesus is the "image of God" and in 2 Cor. 12:8, Paul prays to Christ.[82] By these means, then, Paul does teach the deity of Jesus. This is not a doctrine added by unscrupulous Christians from Rome, but a teaching of Jesus himself and of Paul.

Fourth, even if a divine messiah was not what first century Jews were looking for, there is a good reason why Jesus may still have made this very claim, as the evidence indicates he did. If he was truly deity, then he may have been attempting to correct the first century Jewish understanding of the messiah. And if he was, in fact, raised from the dead, this at least raises the possibility that his claims were verified. Again, any verification of Jesus' teachings is beyond the scope of this book, but if the resurrection is demonstrated as history, then claims in this area can no longer be disregarded.[83] Schonfield might then have to face his thesis in reverse.

At any rate, Schonfield's thesis (as well as others who claim that Jesus' teachings were changed) is invalid. This is especially so when the Gospels have been rejected, for there is then no basis for this conclusion. It is thereby circular to assume that Jesus' views did not differ from first century Jews, for this is the very point to be demonstrated. But then the presumed plot of the Christians at Rome also fails because there is no evidence that Jesus did not teach his own deity. In fact, there is much evidence in the Gospels that he did teach this.

If one rejects the Gospels there is little basis for rejecting the traditional Christian testimony concerning Jesus, and we arrive at a circular argument. If the texts are accepted, then we are faced with Jesus' claims to be deity. Additionally, Paul's firm teaching on the deity of Jesus invalidates this thesis, as does a possible verification of Jesus' claims if his resurrection is demonstrated as historical.

It should be carefully noted, however, that Schonfield and Davies represent only two versions of the thesis that Jesus' message was changed. This claim is a very common one. In general, the frequent charge is that Paul either originated or corrupted Christianity, usually on the subjects of the deity of Jesus and the nature and extent of the gospel message. It is to this more general charge that we wish to offer seven brief critiques.

(1) It has been mentioned above that Jesus made various statements regarding his own deity. He claimed to be the Son of Man, the Son of God, to forgive sin and that he was the actual means of salvation. There are also additional indications of his own teachings concerning his deity, such as his use of the word "Abba." It is quite significant that Jesus' first century contemporaries were convinced of his claim to deity (Mark 2:6-7; John 5:17-18).[84] Therefore, the thesis which asserts that the deity of Jesus is a later doctrine fails largely at this point.

(2) Numerous ancient, pre-Pauline creeds also teach the full deity of Jesus. Philippians 2:6-11 not only attributes Old Testament praise of God (as the one, true God) to Jesus (cf. Isa. 45:22-23), but it also calls Jesus "Christ" and "Lord." On this latter title, Cullmann asserts that it is even loftier than the passages which address Jesus as God, since Lord is the name for God. This allowed Christians to attribute what the Old Testament says about God to Jesus, as evidenced in this passage.[85] Addi-

tionally, and even stronger, Jesus is said in verse six to have the same nature or essence as God. Reginald Fuller states that here Jesus is "equal with God."[86] Cullmann speaks of Jesus' "identity of form with God," which shows that he is "equal with God" in his exaltation.[87] Other pre-Pauline creeds also teach the deity of Jesus. Romans 1:3-4 calls Jesus "Son," "Christ" and "Lord." First Corinthians 11:23ff., which Joachim Jeremias states, "goes back...to Jesus himself,"[88] also calls Jesus "Lord." First Corinthians 15:3ff., perhaps the oldest New Testament creed, calls Jesus "Christ." It is also significant that these creeds pre-date Paul and extend back to the earliest church, which completely compliment Jesus' own self-claims.

(3) Paul did not teach a new religion. He taught that Christianity was a fulfillment of Judaism (Rom. 10:4, 9-11; Col. 2:16-17), which is what Jesus taught, as well (Matt. 5:18; Luke 16:16-17).

(4) Paul also agreed with Jesus as to the nature of the gospel. Both taught that men are sinners (Mark 3:38; Rom. 3:23; 6:23) and that Jesus died, with his shed blood providing atonement for that sin (Matt. 26:28; Mark 10:45; Eph. 1:7; Rom. 5:8). The death and burial of Jesus was completed by his resurrection (Luke 24:46-47; John 20:25-29; Rom. 10:9). Yet man cannot save himself, but needs God's grace and leading (Matt. 19:25-26; John 4:44; Eph. 2:8-9), which is imparted through faith and surrender to Christ (Mark 1:15; John 6:47; Rom. 10:9-11). The result is a changed life and commitment (Luke 14:25-35; John 15:1-11; 2 Cor. 5:17; Eph. 2:10).

(5) Paul was the apostle to the Gentiles (Rom. 11:13-14). Jesus also taught the disciples to take the gospel to the Gentiles (Matt. 28:19-20; Luke 24:47; John 10:16; Acts 1:8) and that non-Jews would be found in the Kingdom of God (Matt. 8:11-12; John 17:20). These teachings are actually the fulfillment of Old Testament promises (Gen. 12:3; Isa. 19:18-25), not a new doctrine.

(6) Paul's message of the gospel was both checked and approved by the original apostles (Gal. 2:1-10), providing official recognition that his message was not opposed to that of Jesus. It was also shown earlier (see Section E) that Paul's epistles were accepted as Scripture immediately after being written (2 Pet. 3:15-16; Clement of Rome; Ignatius and Polycarp).

(7) We have also introduced the significance of Jesus' resurrection with regard to the truthfulness of his teachings. Since Paul agrees with Jesus, any such confirmation would also apply to Paul's teachings.

Therefore we conclude that Paul was not the founder of Christianity and neither did he corrupt Jesus' teachings. They agree on the essentials of the faith. Furthermore, the early pre-Pauline creed in 1 Cor. 15:3ff. presents the same view of the deity of Jesus and the nature of the gospel. As the eminent New Testament scholar C. H. Dodd pointed out, Paul's preaching coincided with that of primitive Christianity and those who would assert otherwise bear the burden of proof.[89]

G. Jesus as international traveller

In surveys of popularistic lives of Jesus, it is not long before one discovers a prevalent tendency to view Jesus as an international traveller. It is sometimes asserted that he took journeys to such places as India, Japan or Egypt during either his eighteen so-called "silent years" (between the ages of twelve and thirty), or trips even after his crucifixion; the latter usually necessitating a swoon theory. We looked briefly at one similar thesis already, with Potter's *The Lost Years of Jesus Revealed*. Although Jesus did not travel overly far, it is taught that he spent his "silent years" in the Qumran community (see Section D above).

Another persistent legend states that Jesus travelled east to India and Japan. According to family documents which were purportedly uncovered in 1935 by Shinto priest Kiyomaro Takeuchi, Jesus reportedly sailed to Japan at the age of eighteen. He stayed in that country for about seven or eight years and studied Japanese philosophy and culture in his search for wisdom. Armed with both this knowledge and with some magic tricks which he learned, Jesus went back to Palestine. Upon his return, Jesus preached the Kingdom of God. When it became clear that he was going to be killed, the Japanese legend relates that his brother, Isukiri, volunteered to die in Jesus' place so that Jesus could continue with his work on earth. Having convinced Jesus by such rationale, his brother Isukiri died and was buried. Afterwards, Jesus and Judas went to the tomb and reburied Isukiri's dead body.

The legend continues by teaching that Jesus then left Palestine and took four years to get to Shinjo, Japan. There he changed his name to Torai Taro Tenkujin, got married and fathered three children. After living a full life as a prophet and teacher, Jesus is said to have died at the age of 112 years. The Japanese of Shinjo commemorated his death with what they claim is Jesus' tomb located in a small valley not far from the village. However, when asked if Jesus is really buried in this tomb,

Shinjo mayor Genki Kosaka replied that he could not say either way.[90]

Another hypothesis involving Jesus as a traveller is related by Donovan Joyce, who asserts that in 1964 he was told of a scroll which was stolen by a professor who would not give him his true name. This professor claimed that the scroll was found at Masada, on the Dead Sea, and was written by a man identifying himself as "Jesus of Gennesareth, son of Jacob," an eighty-year-old defender of Masada who apparently died while fighting the Romans during the Jewish revolt of 66-73 A.D. Unfortunately Joyce never found out the professor's real name and, in the meantime, the scroll has disappeared so that no one knows the whereabouts of it or the professor![91] Yet Joyce claims that there is a chance that this scroll was written by Jesus before his death at the age of eighty years. Therefore, there must be a history of what happened to Jesus during the almost fifty years from the time of his crucifixion until his death.

So Joyce suggests that Jesus never died on the cross, but "plotted" to remain alive in spite of crucifixion. He was drugged on the cross, but the guards, apparently bribed, did not examine Jesus' comatose body too closely. A doctor was concealed in the tomb in order to nurse Jesus back to health again, assisted by Joseph of Arimathea, Jesus's uncle. As Jesus recovered he paid one last visit to his disciples and then retired as a monk at Qumran.[92] But Jesus was not to live out the remainder of his days in the quiet Qumran setting. Joyce postulates that Jesus was a part of the Hasmonean line, and connects him with the Zealots as an open revolutionary against Rome. In accord with this background, Jesus had married Mary Magdalene even before his crucifixion, according to Hasmonean tradition, and fathered at least one son. Jesus was opposed to the Roman rule and left Qumran for Masada, where he died while fighting the Romans.[93]

Another recent attempt to present Jesus as a traveller is the book *Holy Blood, Holy Grail*. Acknowledging the usage of Joyce's presentation, this work also holds that Jesus was married to Mary Magdalene (who is identified as Mary of Bethany). The children from this marriage were heirs of Jesus' kingly bloodline.[94] Jesus was said to have been crucified for crimes perpetrated against Rome, not against the Jews. However, he did not die on the cross, but was drugged to make him appear dead. Pilate was bribed in order to allow Jesus to be removed from the cross alive. The Essenes then took his body, which was laid in the tomb of Joseph of Arimathea, a relative of Jesus. After nursing Jesus back to health, Joseph,

Mary Magdalene and Lazarus (Jesus' brother-in-law) went to France to live. However, no one knows where Jesus went after his recuperation. The authors suggest India, Egypt, Masada or somewhere else in Israel.[95] The vast bulk of the book is devoted to the remains of Jesus' bloodline, through Mary Magdalene, as they settled and spread in France. This supposed bloodline is traced through royal families, secret organizations and age-old mysteries. But, as even the authors recognize, the major question is whether this French lineage did, in fact, come from Jesus.[96]

These attempts to have Jesus avoid death and then travel afterward are ladened with more difficulties than any other approach which we have studied. This is largely due to the presence of so much conjecture combined with an absence of facts. We present four major objections to such approaches to the life of Jesus.

First, in our earlier discussions we determined that the New Testament, and the Gospels in particular, are authentic and trustworthy documents for the life and teachings of Jesus. We will not belabor this point any further, except to note that this conclusion is based on both the early and eyewitness testimony behind the Gospels, including authors who were close to the facts, as well as the attestation of the earliest church and overwhelming manuscript evidence. Such facts reveal that the Gospels are a valid basis for the teachings of Jesus, in opposition to these theses which almost always involve vast alterations of New Testament data. On this point alone these theses fail.

Second, most of these theses involve the swoon theory concerning Jesus' resurrection, without which there would be no basis for any post-crucifixion travels followed by a later, obscure death. But as stated above, this hypothesis falls prey to numerous problems which will not be repeated here (see Section C above).

Some sources, such as the Japanese legend cited here, assert that someone else died on the cross in the place of Jesus. Other such assertions include the gnostic writing "The Second Treatise of the Great Seth (55:15-20)[97] and the Muslim *Koran* (Surah IV, 156-159).[98] Whereas the Japanese tale claims that the crucified person was Jesus' brother, the gnostic source claims that Simon of Cyrene was killed while the glorified Jesus sat in the heavens and laughed at the error. A popular Muslim teaching is that it was Judas who died instead of Jesus.

Such strange "twists" to the swoon theory have been virtually ignored by scholars with good reason, for serious problems invalidate each of these theses. First, the sources which report these theories are quite late.

While the date of the gnostic writing is difficult to obtain, it was probably written two or more centuries after Jesus and definitely manifests theological rather than historical interests, since one gnostic belief is that Jesus could not have died physically on the cross, hence a substitute would be needed. The Japanese legend was not known until about 500 A.D. when it was introduced in Japan by the Chinese. The *Koran* is a seventh century A.D. writing. Works of the third to seventh century are rather late to have much authoritative claim, while the gnostic and Muslim sources plainly exhibit theological interests for their assertions. Second, why would Jesus' disciples, friends and relatives not recognize a substitute, especially when several were present at the crucifixion and burial? This is almost beyond credulity. Third, how could Jesus' enemies have missed the oversight? Since they knew what his appearance was from his trips to Jerusalem and certainly had strong motives to kill him, including the desire to be present at the crucifixion to witness his death, such a mistake would be simply incredible. Finally, such theories would not be able to adequately explain the reported appearances of Jesus to eyewitnesses after his crucifixion, since such testimony concerned both his glorified body and his healed wounds.

It is no wonder that such a variant hypothesis has had very little following even among critics. The late dates of the sources and the lack of recognition by both Jesus' loved ones and his enemies alike, even at extremely close range, together with his glorified but scarred post-crucifixion appearances, combine to make this assertion quite unpalatable to scholars.

The third major objection to the thesis that Jesus was an international traveller after his crucifixion is that these theories lack historical credibility. Each of the theses is plagued with a lack of solid historical evidence. For instance, the Japanese legend not only rests on very questionable heresay testimony but it was not even introduced into Japan until 500 A.D.[99] Certainly a gap of some 450 years should make us question the historical origin of this legend.

Concerning Joyce's thesis that Jesus died at the age of eighty while fighting the Romans at Masada, the historical basis is perhaps even more questionable. Joyce never knew the professor's true name, and even admits that he must rely on "heresay" testimony. If that is not enough, the scroll has since vanished and no one knows the claimed whereabouts of either this document or the "professor" upon whose word the enterprise rests! Interestingly, Joyce even wrote to Yigael Yadin, the well-known archaeologist who headed the Masada expedition. Yadin's response to Joyce's story was that, "anyone with a little knowledge of scrolls and conditions in which they were discovered at Masada would have immediately detected the nonsense in the story."[100] There can be little question that the story of the lost scroll cannot be used in an attempt to formulate the historical facts of the last years of Jesus' life.

In *Holy Blood, Holy Grail* we find a similar gap in the historical basis. The authors themselves characterize their *own* historical argument, before investigating the Christian sources, with the following description:

> Our hypothetical scenario...was also preposterous....much too sketchy ...rested on far too flimsy a foundation....could not yet in itself be supported....too many holes...too many inconsistencies and anomalies, too many loose ends.[101]

After their research into Christian origins, does their evaluation change? While holding that their thesis was still probably true, the authors conclude, "We could not—and still cannot—prove the accuracy of our conclusion. It remains to some extent at least, a hypothesis."[102] As we will see below, their thesis also has numerous gaps in argumentation.

Historically, then, such theses lack the data needed for the conclusions. Very late documents, missing evidence and faulty historical reconstructions certainly do not prove one's case.

The fourth major problem with these theses is that, in addition to the lack of a historical basis, each exhibits decidedly illogical argumentation. The Japanese legend contains such inconsistencies as Jesus' brother dying in his place, the fact that Jesus' teachings reflect none of the Japanese philosophy that he supposedly learned during his "silent years" spent in Japan, and the failure to acknowledge the Christian teachings of Francis Xavier. This Catholic priest visited Japan in the sixteenth century and probably accounts for much of the Christian influence in that country.[103] Even so, it is in the works of Joyce, Baigent, Leigh and Lincoln where we perceive more glaring gaps in logic.

For Joyce, the story does not stop with the admittedly heresay evidence supplied by an anonymous "professor" who disappears along with all of the evidence for his claims, never to be heard from again. After asking where the scroll could have disappeared, Joyce postulates that there is one country in the world which would especially like to discover its contents—Russia! When he arrived in Delhi, India he remembered that the "professor" had also said he was going to Delhi. Therefore, Joyce felt that he had verified his thesis when he spotted a Russian plane at the airport, although he apparently never questioned the presence of planes from various other countries at such an international airport. Russia had to have sent the plane to pick up the "professor" and his valuable scroll![104]

To make matters worse, Joyce claims further evidence for this thesis in that a Russian official held a conference with the Vatican's Pope Paul in 1967. Although there was never a hint of what transpired at this meeting, Joyce is sure that they were talking about the "professor's" scroll! Russia was putting pressure on the Vatican, presumably with world revelation of the scroll hanging in the balances. And after all of this, Joyce states that the still unknown professor is probably a very respected scholar who is no longer free or perhaps even dead, thereby intimating that the Russians have him, so that his story will never be told![105]

Such illogic is also carried over into Joyce's treatment of the life of Jesus. This happens often, but we will recount just one example here. In Luke 8:1-3, we are told that several women supported Jesus and his disciples financially. Joyce declares this to be "quite certain" evidence that Jesus was married.[106] Such a train of illogic hardly needs a comment, but is certainly an example of how such hypotheses must really be strained to put together such a "case" for the life of Jesus. It is also typical of the assertions made in *Holy Blood, Holy Grail*, from which many examples could also be adduced.

It is held that since Jesus and his mother are called to a wedding in John 2:1-11 and since they play a major role, it must therefore automatically be Jesus' own wedding. Apparently no one can play a major role at anyone else's wedding, even if he is able to do miracles![107] In the account of the raising of Lazarus in John 11:1-46, it is asserted that, since Martha ran out to greet Jesus upon his arrival while Mary waited in the house until Jesus asked for her (vv. 20, 28), Mary must be Jesus' wife! The authors even admit a *non sequitur* argument by such reasoning.[108]

It is obvious that, oftentimes in such theses, conclusions are arrived at only by taking out of the Gospels and even adding to them what one would like to find. In this case, the authors even admit this procedure. After stating that they sifted through the Gospels searching for the specific points which they needed, they confessed that, "we would be obliged to read between lines, fill in certain gaps, account for certain caesuras and ellipses. We would have to deal with omissions, with innuendos, with references that were, at best, oblique."[109] One instance of this arbitrary methodology occurs when they admit that they are utilizing such a procedure in order to find evidence for Jesus being married, which is obvious from the above examples on this subject. Another instance follows an attempt to make John the most historical of the four Gospels. The authors assert that modern scholarship has established this point, when such is simply not the case. But the author's motives are exposed when they specifically acknowledge that they used John the most in an attempt to support their hypothesis![110] Thus, we again see examples of illogic being used to support a case for one's own desired results. One is reminded here of Louis Cassels' evaluation of such attempts to "explain away" the facts.

> The amazing thing about all these debunk-Jesus books is that they accept as much of the recorded Gospels as they find convenient, then ignore or repudiate other parts of the same document which contradict their notions.[111]

The trustworthiness of the Gospels, the failure of the swoon theory in all of its forms, the lack of a valid historical basis and the decidedly illogical lines of argumentation demonstrate the failures of these theories. This is not even to mention their hopeless contradiction of one another as well.

H. Summary and conclusion

There have been many popularistic attempts to discredit the Jesus of the Gospels. Even in the eighteenth and nineteenth centuries these attempts were prevalent. While they have been rejected almost unanimously by careful scholars, especially those who remember similar attempts disproven long ago, they still receive widespread attention among lay people. There have even been strictly fictional, novelistic attempts to deal with these subjects.[112]

It is because of this attention among the general populace that we have considered these popularistic "lives of Jesus" in this chapter. Accordingly, we investigated hypotheses involving swoon, Qumran connections, gnostic syncretism, perversions of Jesus' message and theses involving Jesus as an international traveller. Each was refuted on its own grounds by a number of criticisms.

Louis Cassels responded rather harshly to such "debunking" attempts:

You can count on it. Every few years, some 'scholar' will stir up a short-lived sensation by publishing a book that says something outlandish about Jesus.

The 'scholar' usually has no standing as a Bible student, theologian, archeologist, or anything else related to serious religious study.

But that need not hold him back. If he has a job—any job—on a university faculty, his 'findings' will be treated respectfully in the press as a 'scholarly work.'[113]

Although such satirical comments remind one of Schweitzer's similar remarks concerning the "imperfectly equipped free-lances" who composed the "fictitious lives of Jesus" from 130 to 200 years ago,[114] these statements cannot fairly be applied to all of the writings in this chapter. Yet they do remind us of characteristics which are true of many. Accordingly, while all of the books surveyed in this chapter are refuted by the facts, some of them are additionally to be viewed from the standpoint of fictitious attempts to avoid the Jesus of the Gospels.

Notes

[1]Schweitzer, *The Quest of the Historical Jesus*, p. 38.
[2]Ibid.
[3]Ibid., pp. 39-44.
[4]Ibid., pp. 44-47.
[5]Ibid., pp. 161-166.
[6]Schonfield (New York: Bantam Books, 1965).
[7]Ibid., pp. 37-38.
[8]Ibid., pp. 112-115.
[9]Ibid., pp. 153-161.
[10]Ibid., pp. 160-161.
[11]Ibid., p. 165.
[12]Ibid., pp. 166-172.
[13]Ibid., p. 6.
[14]Ibid., p. 165; cf. pp. 171-173.
[15]J. A. T. Robinson, *Can We Trust the New Testament?*, p. 15.
[16]Joyce (New York: New American Library, 1972).
[17]Ibid., pp. 106-110, 118

[18]David Strauss, *A New Life of Jesus*, 2 vols. (Edinburgh: Williams and Norgate, 1879), vol. 1, pp. 408-412.

[19]Schweitzer, pp. 56-67.

[20]Ibid., cf. pp. 161-166 with 166-179, for example.

[21]Eduard Riggenbach, *The Resurrection of Jesus* (New York: Eaton and Mains, 1907), pp. 48-49; James Orr, p. 92.

[22]For examples of physicians who deal with this issue, see C. Truman Davis, "The Crucifixion of Jesus: The Passion of Christ from a Medical Point of View," in *Arizona Medicine*, March, 1965, pp. 183-187; Robert Wassenar, "A Physician Looks at the Suffering of Christ" in *Moody Monthly*, 79/7, March 1979, pp. 41-42; James H. Jewell, Jr., and Patricia A. Didden, "A Surgeon Looks at the Cross," in *Voice*, 58/2, March-April, 1979, pp. 3-5.

[23]For examples, Barth, *Church Dogmatics*, vol. IV, p. 340 and Brown, p. 223.

[24]Ewing (New York: Philosophical Library, 1961).

[25]Ibid., pp. 48-51, 62-63.

[26]Ibid., pp. 52, 62-64.

[27]Ibid., see pp. 62-64, 368-369, 393, 397, for examples.

[28]Charles Potter, *The Lost Years of Jesus Revealed* (Greenwich: Fawcett Publications, Inc., n.d.).

[29]Charles Potter, *Did Jesus Write This Book?* (Greenwich: Fawcett Publications, Inc., 1965), pp. 16, 77, 133-141.

[30]Ewing, p. 51.

[31]Ibid., p. 78.

[32]Potter, *Did Jesus Write This Book?*, p. 14.

[33]Ibid., pp. 134-135.

[34]Ibid., p. 136.

[35]Jean Daniélou, "What the Dead Sea Scrolls Tell Us About Jesus," in Daniel-Rops, *Sources for Christ*, pp. 23-28; John M. Allegro, *The Dead Sea Scrolls* (Baltimore: Penguin Books, 1956), pp. 148-151; William Brownlee, "Jesus and Qumran," in *Jesus and the Historian*, ed. by F. Thomas Trotter (Philadelphia: The Westminster Press, 1968), p. 75.

[36]Brownlee, p. 52.

[37]Daniélou, pp. 28-29; Allegro, pp. 161-162; Brownlee, pp. 62-76; Charles Pfeiffer, *The Dead Sea Scrolls and the Bible* (Grand Rapids: Baker Book House, 1969), pp. 97-99, 130-134; F. F. Bruce, *Second Thoughts on the Dead Sea Scrolls* (Grand Rapids: William B. Eerdmans Publishing Company, 1956), pp. 79-84.

[38]Allegro, p. 160.

[39]Daniélou, p. 28.

[40]Daniélou, pp. 30-32; Brownlee, pp. 69-70; Allegro, pp. 161-162; Bruce, *Second Thoughts*, p. 98.

[41]Pfeiffer, p. 97.

[42]Although this argument cannot be pursued here, see Habermas, *The Resurrection of Jesus: An Apologetic*

[43]James M. Robinson, editor, *The Nag Hammadi Library* (New York: Harper and Row, Publishers, 1977), pp. 37, 98, 117, for examples.

[44]Elaine Pagels, *The Gnostic Gospels* (New York: Random House, 1979), pp. XXII-XXIV.

[45]Ibid., pp. 20, 177-178.

[46]Ibid., pp. 12-13, 84-90.

[47]Ibid., pp. 170-171, 180-181.

[48]A. Powell Davies, *The Meaning of the Dead Sea Scrolls* (New York: The New American Library, 1956), especially p. 120. Incidently, Davies also asserts that Jesus is not the Essene "Teacher of Righteousness," who cannot be identified with any great amount of assurance (pp. 73-74).

[49]Ibid., p. 126; cf. p. 120.

[50]Pagels, pp. XXIII-XXIV, 20.

[51]Ibid., pp. 20-21.

[52]Archibald M. Hunter, *Bible and Gospel* (Philadelphia: The Westminster Press, 1969), pp. 29-32; Daniel-Rops, pp. 21, 38, 50-85; Francois Amiot, "Jesus, An Historical Person," in Daniel-Rops, p. 10; Grant, pp. 180; cf. pp. 199-200.

[53]C. E. B. Cranfield, *The Gospel According to Mark* (Cambridge: Cambridge University Press, 1963), pp. 5-6; A. M. Hunter, *The Gospel According to St. Mark* (London: SCM Press LTD, 1953), pp. 16-17; A. M. Hunter, *Introducing the New Testament*, pp. 41-43; Robert M. Grant, *An Historical Introduction to the New Testament*, p. 119; F. F. Bruce, *The New Testament Documents*, pp. 35-37; R. A. Cole, *The Gospel According to St. Mark* (Grand Rapids: William B. Eerdmans Publishing Company, 1970), pp. 28-50.

[54]Hunter, *Introducing the New Testament*, pp. 55-56; Robert Grant, p. 129; Bruce, *The New Testament Documents*, pp. 39-40.

[55]Noryal Geldenhuys, *Commentary on the Gospel of Luke* (Grand Rapids: William B. Eerdmans Publishing Company, 1972), pp. 15-22; E. J. Tinsley, *The Gospel According to Luke* (Cambridge: Cambridge University Press, 1965), pp. 2-4; C. F. D. Moule, *Christ's Messengers: Studies in Acts of the Apostles* (New York: Association Press, 1957), pp. 10-13; Hunter, *Introducing the New Testament*, pp. 49-50; William Hamilton, *The Modern Reader's Guide to Matthew and Luke* (New York: Association Press, 1957), p. 14; Robert Grant, pp. 134-135; F. F. Bruce, *Commentary on the Book of Acts* (Grand Rapids: William B. Eerdmans Publishing Company, 1971), p. 19; *The New Testament Documents*, pp. 41-44; Ray Summers, *Commentary on Luke* (Waco: Word Books, Publisher, 1972), pp. 8-10.

[56]Raymond E. Brown, *New Testament Essays* (Milwaukee: The Bruce Publishing Company, 1965), pp. 129-131; Leon Morris, *The Gospel According to John* (Grand Rapids: William B. Eerdmans Publishing Company, 1971), pp. 8-35; R. V. G. Tasker, *The Gospel According to St. John* (Grand Rapids: William B. Eerdmans Publishing Company, 1968), pp. 11-20; Hunter, *Introducing the New Testament*, pp. 61-63; Robert Grant, p. 160; William Hamilton, *The Modern Reader's*

Guide to John (New York: Association Press, 1959), pp. 13-15; Robinson, p. 83; Bruce, *The New Testament Documents*, pp. 48-49.

[57]For details on these points, see Hunter, *Bible and Gospel*, pp. 32-37.

[58]Brownlee, pp. 75-76; Allegro, p. 128; Helmbold, pp. 89-90; Bruce, *The New Testament Documents*, p. 58.

[59]Pagels, *Gnostic Gospels*, pp. 177-178.

[60] Ibid., pp. XXIII-XXIV.

[61]The division citations in the following references, as well as the translation, are taken from J. B. Lightfoot, editor and translator, *The Apostolic Fathers* (Grand Rapids: Baker Book House, 1971).

[62]Papias is not the only early Christian source to refer to the gospel of John. We find possible allusions to this gospel in Clement's "Corinthians" (43) and Ignatius' "Ephesians" (5, 17). It is definitely referred to by Justin Martyr (ca. 150 A.D.). It is also included in Tatian's fourfold gospel (about 170 A.D.) and in the Muratorian Canon (about 180 A.D.).

[63]See Helmbold, pp. 88-89.

[64]Pagels, pp. 170-171.

[65]Hugh Schonfield, *Those Incredible Christians* (New York: Bantam Books, 1969), pp. IX, 50-51.

[66]Ibid., p. 67.

[67]Ibid., pp. 135-155.

[68]Ibid., pp. 136-149.

[69]Ibid., pp. 149, 211, 230.

[70]Ibid., pp. XVII, 170.

[71]Ibid., pp. 142-146, 259-272.

[72]Ibid., pp. 50-51.

[73]See Habermas, *The Resurrection of Jesus: An Apologetic*, Chapter 3 for several additional indications of Jesus' claims to deity.

[74]Reginald Fuller, *The Foundations of New Testament Christology* (New York: Charles Scribner's Sons, 1965), p. 115, for instance.

[75]Schonfield, *Those Incredible Christians*, pp. 98, 257.

[76]Ibid., p. 155.

[77]Oscar Cullmann, *The Christology of the New Testament*, transl. by Shirley Guthrie and Charles Hall (Philadelphia: The Westminster Press, 1963), pp. 311-312.

[78]Ibid., pp. 312-313; Raymond E. Brown, *Jesus: God and Man* (Milwaukee: The Bruce Publishing Company, 1967), pp. 20-22.

[79]Schonfield, *Those Incredible Christians*, p. 252.

[80]Cullmann, p. 311.

[81]A. T. Robinson, *Word Pictures in the New Testament*, 6 vols. (Nashville: Broadman Press, 1931), vol. 4, p. 491.

[82]Cullmann, pp. 235, 311-312.

[83]See Habermas, *The Ressurrection of Jesus: An Apologetic*, especially chapters 1-3 for the details of such an argument.

[84]The subject of Jesus' self-designations is an intricate issue and cannot be dealt with in any detail here. For some justification of these claims, see Oscar Cullmann, *The Christology of the New Testament*. On the last point, see Reginald Fuller, p. 115.

[85]Cullmann, pp. 235, 237, 307.

[86]Fuller, pp. 208, 248.

[87]Cullmann, pp. 321; see also p. 235.

[88]Joachim Jeremias, *The Eucharistic Words of Jesus*, transl. by Norman Perrin (London: SCM Press, LTD, 1966), p. 101.

[89]C. H. Dodd, *The Apostolic Preaching and its Developments* (Grand Rapids: Baker Book House, 1980), p. 16.

[90]John Peterson, "A Legend Says Jesus Died in Japan at 112," *The Detroit News*, August 9, 1971, pp. 1A, 6A. There are other parallels of a similar nature in Ethiopia and Egypt.

[91]Joyce, *The Jesus Scroll*, pp. 7-14.

[92]Ibid., pp. 100-110, 131-140, 160.

[93]Ibid., pp. 54-59, 76-99, 141-158.

[94]Michael Baigent, Richard Leigh and Henry Lincoln, *Holy Blood, Holy Grail* (New York: Delacorte Press, 1982), pp. 301-320, 324.

[95]Ibid., pp. 322-332, 347.

[96]Ibid., see Chapters 1-11, 13 for details. See p. 286 for the author's statement concerning the need to have evidence of such a bloodline.

[97]See James Robinson, *The Nag Hammadi Library*, pp. 329-338.

[98]*The Meaning of the Glorious Koran*, transl. by Mohammed Marmaduke Pickthall (New York: New American Library, n.d.), p. 93.

[99]Peterson, p. 6A.

[100]Joyce, p. 187; see also pp. 7-14.

[101]Baigent, Leigh and Lincoln, p. 286.

[102]Ibid., p. 372

[103]Peterson, p. 6A.

[104]Joyce, pp. 158-159, 184.

[105]Ibid., pp. 159-160, 191.

[106]Ibid., pp. 78-79.

[107]Baigent, Leigh and Lincoln, pp. 303-304.

[108]Ibid., pp. 307-308.

[109]Ibid., p. 103.

[110]Ibid.

[111]Louis Cassels, "Debunkers of Jesus Still Trying," *The Detroit News*, June 23, 1973, p. 7A.

[112]Templeton, *Act of God*; Irving Wallace, *The Word* (New York: Pocket Books,

1973); Og Mandino, *The Christ Commission* (New York: Bantam Books, Inc., 1981).

[113]Cassels, p. 7A.

[114]Schweitzer, *The Quest of the Historical Jesus*, p. 38.

PART TWO

*Historical Data Concerning
Jesus' Life*

4

Ancient Non-Christian Sources

Beginning our historical investigation into the early sources for the life, death and resurrection of Jesus, we turn first to the ancient non-Christian sources. We will move, successively from ancient historians, to government officials, to other Jewish and Gentile sources, to early gnostic sources and then to lost works which speak of Jesus. A synopsis of this data will conclude this chapter.

A. Ancient historians

Tacitus. Cornelius Tacitus (ca. 55-120 A.D.) was a Roman historian who lived through the reigns of over a half dozen Roman emperors. He has been called the "greatest historian" of ancient Rome, an individual generally acknowledged among scholars for his moral "integrity and essential goodness."[1]

Tacitus is best known for two works—the *Annals* and the *Histories*. The former is thought to have included eighteen books and the latter to have included twelve, for a total of thirty.[2] The *Annals* cover the period from Augustus' death in 14 A.D. to that of Nero in 68 A.D., while the *Histories* begin after Nero's death and proceed to that of Domitian in 96 A.D.

Tacitus recorded at least one reference to Christ and two to early Christianity, one in each of his major works. The most important one is found in the *Annals*, written about 115 A.D. The following was recounted concerning the great fire in Rome during the reign of Nero:

Consequently, to get rid of the report, Nero fastened the guilt and inflicted the most exquisite tortures on a class hated for their abominations, called Christians by the populace. Christus, from whom the name had its origin, suffered the extreme penalty during the reign of Tiberius at the hands of one of our procurators, Pontius Pilatus, and a most mischievous superstition, thus checked for the moment, again broke out not only in Judaea, the first source of the evil, but even in Rome, where all things hideous and shameful from every part of the world find their centre and become popular. Accordingly, an arrest was first made of all who pleaded guilty; then, upon their information, an immense multitude was convicted, not so much of the crime of firing the city, as of hatred against mankind. Mockery of every sort was added to their deaths. Covered with the skins of beasts, they were torn by dogs and perished, or were nailed to crosses, or were doomed to the flames and burnt, to serve as a nightly illumination, when daylight had expired.

Nero offered his gardens for the spectacle, and was exhibiting a show in the circus, while he mingled with the people in the dress of a charioteer or stood aloft on a car. Hence, even for criminals who deserved extreme and exemplary punishment, there arose a feeling of compassion; for it was not, as it seemed, for the public good, but to glut one man's cruelty, that they were being destroyed.[3]

From this report we can learn several facts, both explicit and implicit, concerning Christ and the Christians who lived in Rome in the 60s A.D. Chronologically, we may ascertain the following information.

(1) Christians were named after their founder, Christus (from the Latin), (2) who was put to death by the Roman procurator Pontius Pilatus (also Latin), (3) during the reign of emperor Tiberius (14-37 A.D.). (4) His death ended the "superstition" for a short time, (5) but it broke out again, (6) especially in Judaea, where the teaching had its origin.

(7) His followers carried his doctrine to Rome. (8) When the great fire destroyed a large part of the city during the reign of Nero (54-68 A.D.), the emperor placed the blame on the Christians who lived in Rome. (9) Tacitus reports that this group was hated for their abominations. (10) These Christians were arrested after pleading guilty, (11) and many were convicted of "hatred for mankind." (12) They were mocked and (13) then tortured, including being "nailed to crosses" or burnt to death. (14) Because of these actions, the people had compassion on the Christians. (15) Tacitus therefore concluded that such punishments were not for public good but were simply "to glut one man's cruelty."[4]

Several facts here are of interest. As F. F. Bruce has noted, Tacitus had to receive his information from some source and this may have been an official record. It may even have been contained in one of Pilate's reports to the emperor, to which Tacitus would probably have had access because of his standing with the government.[5] Of course, we cannot be sure at this point, but a couple of early writers do claim to know the contents of such a report, as we will perceive later.

Also of interest is the historical context for Jesus' death, as he is linked with both Pilate and Tiberius. Additionally, J. N. D. Anderson, of the University of London, sees implications in Tacitus' quote concerning Jesus' resurrection. He states:

> It is scarcely fanciful to suggest that when he adds that 'A most mischievous superstition, thus checked for the moment, again broke out' he is bearing indirect and unconscious testimony to the conviction of the early church that the Christ who had been crucified had risen from the grave.[6]

Although we must be careful not to press this implication too far, the possibility remains that Tacitus may have indirectly referred to the Christians' belief in Jesus' resurrection, since his teachings "again broke out" after his death.

Also interesting is the mode of torture employed against the early Christians. Besides burning, a number were crucified by being "nailed to crosses." Not only is this the method used with Jesus, but tradition reports that Nero was responsible for crucifying Peter as well, but upside down. The compassion aroused in the Roman people is also noteworthy.

The second reference to Jesus in the writings of Tacitus is found in his *Histories*. While the specific reference is lost, as is most of this book, the reference is preserved by Sulpicus Severus.[7] He informs us that Tacitus wrote of the burning of the Jerusalem temple by the Romans in 70 A.D., an event which destroyed the city. The Christians are mentioned as a group that were connected with these events. All we can gather from this reference is that Tacitus was also aware of the existence of Christians other than in the context of their presence in Rome. Granted, the facts that Tacitus (and most other extra-biblical sources) report about Jesus are well known in our present culture. Yet we find significance in the surprising confirmation for the life of Jesus.

Suetonius. Another Roman historian who also makes one reference to Jesus and one to Christians is Gaius Suetonius Tranquillas. Little is known about him except that he was the chief secretary of Emperor Hadrian (117-138 A.D.) and that he had access to the imperial records.[8] The first reference occurs in the section on emperor Claudius (41-54

A.D.). Writing about the same time as Tacitus,[9] Suetonius remarked concerning Claudius:

> Because the Jews at Rome caused continuous disturbances at the instigation of Chrestus, he expelled them from the city.[10]

The translator notes that "Chrestus" is a variant spelling of "Christ," as noted by other commentators as well,[11] and is virtually the same as Tacitus' Latin spelling.

Suetonius refers to a wave of riots which broke out in a large Jewish community in Rome during the year of 49 A.D. As a result, the Jews were banished from the city. Incidently, this statement has an interesting corroboration in Acts 18:2, which relates that Paul met a Jewish couple from Pontus named Aquila and his wife Priscilla, who had recently left Italy because Claudius had demanded that all Jews leave Rome.

The second reference from Suetonius is again to the Christians who were tortured by emperor Nero:

> After the great fire at Rome....Punishments were also inflicted on the Christians, a sect professing a new and mischievous religious belief.[12]

Few facts are derived from the two references by Suetonius. The first relates (1) to the expulsion of Jews from Rome, but also makes the claim (2) that it was Christ who caused the Jews to make the uproar in Rome, apparently by his teachings. The second reference is quite similar to the longer statement by Tacitus, (3) including the use of the word "mischievous" to describe the group's beliefs and (4) the term "Christians" to identify this group as followers of the teachings of Christ.

Josephus. Jewish historian Flavius Josephus was born in 37 or 38 A.D. and died in 97 A.D. He was born into a priestly family and became a Pharisee at the age of nineteen. After surviving a battle against the Romans, he served commander Vespasian in Jerusalem. After the destruction of Jerusalem in 70 A.D., he moved to Rome, where he became the court historian for emperor Vespasian.[13]

The *Antiquities*, one of Josephus' major works, provides some valuable but disputed evidence concerning Jesus. Written around 90-95 A.D., it is earlier than the testimonies of the Roman historians. Josephus speaks about many persons and events of first century Palestine and makes two references to Jesus. The first is very brief and is in the context of a reference to James, "the brother of Jesus, who was called Christ."[14] Here we find a close connection between Jesus and James and the belief on the part of some that Jesus was the Messiah.

The second reference is easily the most important and the most debated, since some of the words appear to be due to Christian interpolation. For instance, a portion of the quotation reports:

> Now, there was about this time Jesus, a wise man, if it be lawful to call him a man. For he was one who wrought surprising feats....He was (the) Christ...he appeared to them alive again the third day, as the divine prophets had foretold these and ten thousand other wonderful things concerning him.[15]

Since Josephus was a Jew, it is unlikely that he would have written about Jesus in this way. Origen relates that Josephus did not believe Jesus to be the Messiah,[16] yet Eusebius quotes the debated passage including the words above.[17] Therefore, some commentators believe that this portion is a Christian interpolation. Yet some well-known scholars such as Harnack supported the original ending.[18] A mediating position taken by many holds that the passage itself is written by Josephus with the questionable words either deleted or modified. So the major question here concerns ascertaining the actual words of Josephus.

There are good indications that the majority of the text is genuine. There is no textual evidence against it, and, conversely, there is very good manuscript evidence for this statement about Jesus, thus making it difficult to ignore. Additionally, leading scholars on the works of Josephus have testified that this portion is written in the style of this Jewish historian.[19] Thus we conclude that there are good reasons for accepting this version of Josephus' statement about Jesus, with modifications of the questionable words. In fact, it is possible that these modifications can even be accurately ascertained.

In 1972 Professor Schlomo Pines of the Hebrew University in Jerusalem released the results of a study on an Arabic manuscript containing Josephus' statement about Jesus. It includes a different and briefer rendering of the entire passage, including changes in the key words listed above:

> At this time there was a wise man who was called Jesus. And his conduct was good and (he) was known to be virtuous. And many people from among the Jews and other nations became his disciples. Pilate condemned him to be crucified and to die. And those who had become his

disciples did not abandon his discipleship. They reported that he had appeared to them three days after his crucifixion and that he was alive; accordingly, he was perhaps the messiah concerning whom the prophets
have recounted wonders.[20]

Of the three disputed portions, none remains unchanged. The initial
problematical statement "if it be lawful to call him a man" has been
dropped completely, recounting only that Jesus was a wise man. The
words "he was a doer of wonderful works" have also been deleted. Instead of the words "He was (the) Christ" we find "he was perhaps the
messiah." The phrase "he appeared to them the third day" now reads
"they (the disciples) reported that he had appeared to them," which is an
entirely true statement which was voiced by the first century eyewitnesses. Lastly, the statement that "the divine prophets had foretold
these and ten thousand other wonderful things concerning him" has
been drastically reduced to "concerning whom the prophets have recounted wonders," which concerns the messiah and possibly not even
Jesus, according to Josephus. Therefore, while some words are completely deleted, others are qualified by "perhaps" and "reported."

There are some good reasons why the Arabic version may indeed be
the original words of Josephus before any Christian interpolations. As
Schlomo Pines and David Flusser, of the Hebrew University, have
stated, it is quite plausible that none of the arguments against Josephus
writing the original words even applies to the Arabic text, especially
since the latter would have had less chance of being censored by the
church. In addition, Flusser notes that an earmark of authenticity comes
from the fact that the Arabic version omits the accusation that the Jews
were to blame for Jesus' death, which is included in the original reading.[21]

We conclude that Josephus did write about Jesus, not only in the brief
statement concerning James, but also in this longer account. The evidence points to his composition of this latter passage with the deletion
and modification of a number of key phrases which were probably inter-
polated by Christian sources.

What historical facts can be ascertained from the deleted and altered
portions of Josephus' statement such as those changes made in the Arabic version? (1) Jesus was known as a wise and virtuous man, one recognized for his good conduct. (2) He had many disciples, both Jews and
Gentiles. (3) Pilate condemned him to die, with crucifixion explicitly

being mentioned as the mode. (4) The disciples reported that Jesus had risen from the dead and that he had appeared to them on the third day after his crucifixion. (5) Consequently, the disciples continued to proclaim his teachings. (6) Perhaps Jesus was the Messiah concerning whom the Old Testament prophets spoke and predicted wonders. We would add here two facts from Josephus' earlier quotation as well. (7) Jesus was the brother of James and (8) was called the messiah by some.[22]

There is nothing really sensational in such a list of facts from a Jewish historian. Jesus' ethical conduct, his following, and his crucifixion by the command of Pilate are what we would expect a historian to mention. Even the account of the disciples' report of Jesus' resurrection has an especially authentic note to it in that Josephus, like many historians today, would simply be recounting the claims of the disciples, which were probably fairly well known in first century Palestine. That the disciples would then spread his teachings would be a natural consequence.

Josephus presented an important account of several major facts about Jesus and the origins of Christianity. In spite of some question as to the exact wording of his original writing, we can view his statements as providing probable attestation, in particular, to the death of Jesus by crucifixion, the disciples' report of his resurrection and their subsequent teaching of Jesus' message.

Thallus. At least the death of Jesus was mentioned in an ancient history composed many years before Tacitus, Suetonius or Josephus ever wrote and probably even prior to the Gospels. Circa 52 A.D. Thallus wrote a history of the Eastern Mediterranean world from the Trojan War to his own time.[23] This work itself has been lost and only fragments of it exist in the citations of others. One such scholar who knew and spoke of it was Julius Africanus, who wrote around 221 A.D. It is debated whether he was the same one referred to by Josephus as a wealthy Samaritan, who was made a freedman by Emperor Tiberius and who loaned money to Herod Agrippa I.[24]

In speaking of Jesus' crucifixion and the darkness that covered the land during this event, Africanus found a reference in the writings of Thallus which dealt with this cosmic report. Africanus asserts:

> Thallus, in the third book of his histories, explains away the darkness as
> an eclipse of the sun—unreasonably, as it seems to me.[25]

Julius Africanus objected to Thallus' rationalization concerning the darkness which fell on the land at the time of the crucifixion because an eclipse could not take place during the time of the full moon, as was the case during the Jewish Passover season.[26]

From this brief statement by Thallus we can ascertain that (1) the Christian gospel, or at least an account of the crucifixion of Jesus, was known in the Mediterranean region by the middle of the first century A.D. This brings to mind the presence of Christian teachings in Rome mentioned by Tacitus and Suetonius. (2) Unbelievers offered rationalistic explanations for certain Christian teachings or for supernatural claims not long after their initial proclamation, a point to which we will return below.

B. Government officials

Pliny the Younger. A Roman author and administrator who served as the governor of Bithynia in Asia Minor, Pliny the Younger was the nephew and adopted son of a natural historian known as Pliny the Elder. The younger Pliny is best known for his letters, and Bruce refers to him as "one of the world's great letter-writers, whose letters...have attained the status of literary classics."[27]

Ten books of Pliny's correspondence are extant today. The tenth book, written around 112 A.D., speaks about Christianity in the province of Bithynia and also provides some facts about Jesus.[28] Pliny found that the Christian influence was so strong that the pagan temples had been nearly deserted, pagan festivals severely decreased and the sacrificial animals had few buyers. Because of the inflexibility of Christians and the emperor's prohibition against political association, governor Pliny took action against the Christians. Yet, because he was unsure of how to deal with believers, if there should be any distinctions in treatment or if repentance made any difference, he wrote to Emperor Trajan to explain his approach.

Pliny dealt personally with the Christians who were turned over to him. He interrogated them, inquiring if they were believers. If they answered in the affirmative he asked them two more times, under the threat of death. If they continued firm in their belief, he ordered them to be executed. Sometimes the punishment included torture to obtain desired information, as in the case of two female slaves who were deaconesses in the church. If the person was a Roman citizen, they were sent to the emperor in Rome for trial. If they denied being Christians or had disavowed their faith in the past, they "repeated after me an invoca-tion to the Gods, and offered adoration...to your [Trajan's] image." Af-terwards they "finally cursed Christ." Pliny explained that his purpose in all this was that "multitudes may be reclaimed from error."[29]

Since Pliny's letter is rather lengthy, we will quote the portion which pertains directly to an account of early Christian worship of Christ:

> They (the Christians) were in the habit of meeting on a certain fixed day before it was light, when they sang in alternate verses a hymm to Christ, as to a god, and bound themselves by a solemn oath, not to any wicked deeds, but never to commit any fraud, theft or adultery, never to falsify their word, nor deny a trust when they should be called upon to deliver it up; after which it was their custom to separate, and then reassemble to partake of food—but food of an ordinary and innocent kind.[30]

At this point Pliny adds that Christianity attracted persons of all soci-etal ranks, all ages, both sexes and from both the city and the country.

From Pliny's letter we find several more facts about Jesus and early Christianity. (1) Christ was worshipped as deity by early believers. (2) Pliny refers late in his letter to the teachings of Jesus and his followers as "excessive superstition" and "contagious superstition," which is reminis-cent of the words of both Tacitus and Suetonius. (3) Jesus' ethical teach-ings are reflected in the oath taken by Christians never to be guilty of any of a number of sins mentioned in the letter. (4) We find a probable reference to Christ's institution of communion and the Christian cele-bration of the "love feast" in Pliny's remark about their regathering to partake of ordinary food. The reference here alludes to the accusation on the part of non-Christians that believers were suspected of ritual murder and drinking of blood during these meetings, again confirming our view that communion is the subject to which Pliny is referring. (5) There is also a possible reference to Sunday worship in Pliny's statement that Christians met "on a certain day."

Concerning early Christianity, (6) we see Pliny's method of dealing with believers, from their identification, to their interrogation, to their execution. For those who denied being Christians, worship of the gods and the emperor gained them their freedom. (7) Interestingly, Pliny re-ports that true believers could not be forced to worship the gods or the emperor. (8) Christian worship involved a pre-dawn service, (9) which included singing hymns. The early time probably facilitated a normal working day. (10) These Christians apparently formed a typical cross-

95

section of society in Bithynia, since they were of all classes, ages, localities and of both sexes. (11) There were recognized positions in the church, as illustrated by the mention of the two female deaconesses who were tortured for information. While Pliny does not relate many facts about Jesus, he does provide a look at a very early example of Christian worship. Believers were meeting regularly and worshipping Jesus.

Emperor Trajan. Pliny's inquiry received a reply which is published along with his letters, although Emperor Trajan's response is much shorter:

> The method you have pursued, my dear Pliny, in sifting the cases of those denounced to you as Christians is extremely proper. It is not possible to lay down any general rule which can be applied as the fixed standard in all cases of this nature. No search should be made for these people; when they are denounced and found guilty they must be punished; with the restriction, however, that when the party denies himself to be a Christian, and shall give proof that he is not (that is, by adoring our Gods) he shall be pardoned on the ground of repentance, even though he may have formerly incurred suspicion. Informations without the accuser's name subscribed must not be admitted in evidence against anyone, as it is introducing a very dangerous precedent, and by no means agreeable to the spirit of the age.[31]

Trajan responds that Pliny was generally correct in his actions. If confessed Christians persist in their faith, they must be punished. However, three restrictions are placed on Pliny. (1) Christians should not be sought out or tracked down. (2) Repentance coupled with worship of the gods sufficed to clear a person. Pliny expressed doubts as to whether a person should be punished in spite of repentance and only recounts the pardoning of persons who had willingly given up their beliefs prior to their questioning. (3) Pliny was not to honor any lists of Christians which were given to him if the accuser did not name himself.

These conditions imposed by emperor Trajan give us some insight into early official Roman views about Christianity. While persecution was certainly an issue and many Christians died without committing any actual crimes, it is interesting that, contrary to popular opinion, the first century was not the worst period of persecution for believers. Trajan's restrictions on Pliny at least indicate that it was not a wholesale slaughter. Nonetheless, the persecution was real and many died for their faith.

Emperor Hadrian. The existence of trials for Christians, such as the ones held in the time of Pliny, is confirmed by another historical reference to Christians. Serenius Granianus, proconsul of Asia, wrote to emperor Hadrian (117-138 A.D.), also in reference to the treatment of believers. Hadrian replied to Minucius Fundanus, the successor as Asian proconsul and issued a statement against those who would accuse Christians falsely or without due process. In the letter, preserved by third century church historian Eusebius, Hadrian asserts:

> I do not wish, therefore, that the matter should be passed by without examination, so that these men may neither be harassed, nor opportunity of malicious proceedings be offered to informers. If, therefore, the provincials can clearly evince their charges against the Christians, so as to answer before the tribunal, let them pursue this course only, but not by mere petitions, and mere outcries against the Christians. For it is far more proper, if any one would bring an accusation, that you should examine it.[32]

Hadrian explains that, if Christians are found guilty, after an examination, they should be judged "according to the heinousness of the crime." Yet, if the accusers were only slandering the believers, then those who inaccurately made the charges were to be punished.[33]

From Hadrian's letter we again ascertain (1) that Christians were frequently reported as lawbreakers in Asia and were punished in various ways. (2) Like Trajan, Hadrian also encouraged a certain amount of temperance, and ordered that Christians not be harassed. (3) If Christians were indeed guilty, as indicated by careful examination, punishments could well be in order. (4) However, no undocumented charges were to be brought against believers and those engaged in such were to be punished themselves.

C. Other Jewish sources

The Talmud. The Jews handed down a large amount of oral tradition from generation to generation. This material was organized according to subject matter by Rabbi Akiba before his death in 135 A.D. His work was then revised by his student, Rabbi Meir. The project was completed about 200 A.D. by Rabbi Judah and is known as the Mishnah. Ancient commentary on the Mishnah was called the Gemaras. The combination of the Mishnah and the Gemaras form the Talmud.[34]

It would be expected that the most reliable information about Jesus

from the Talmud would come from the earliest period of compilation—
70 to 200 A.D., known as the Tannaitic period. A very significant quotation is found in Sanhedrin 43a, dating from just this early period:

> On the eve of the Passover Yeshu was hanged. For forty days before the ex-
> ecution took place, a herald went forth and cried, 'He is going forth to be
> stoned because he has practised sorcery and enticed Israel to apostacy.
> Any one who can say anything in his favour, let him come forward and
> plead on his behalf.' But since nothing was brought forward in his favour
> he was hanged on the eve of the Passover![35]

Here we have another brief account of the death of Jesus. These two references to Jesus being "hanged" certainly provide an interesting term to
describe his death. But it should be noted that the New Testament
speaks of crucifixion in the same way. Jesus is said to have been
"hanged" (Greek *kremámenos* in Gal. 3:13), as were the two males killed
at the same time (Greek *kremasthentōn* in Luke 23:39). While the term
"crucified" is a much more common reference to this event,[36] "hanged"
is a variant expression of the same fate.

From this passage in the Talmud we learn about (1) the fact of Jesus'
death by crucifixion and (2) the time of this event, which is mentioned
twice as occurring on the eve of the Jewish Passover. We are surprisingly
told (3) that for forty days beforehand it was publically announced that
Jesus would be stoned. While not specifically recorded in the New Testament, such is certainly consistent with both Jewish practice and with
the report that this had also been threatened on at least two other occasions (John 8:58-59; 10:31-33, 39). It is related (4) that Jesus was judged
by the Jews to be guilty of "sorcery" and spiritual apostasy in leading Israel astray by his teaching. (5) It is also stated that since no witnesses
came forward to defend him, he was killed.

It is interesting that there is no explanation as to why Jesus was crucified ("hanged") when stoning was the prescribed punishment. It is likely
that the Roman involvement provided the "change of plans," without
specifically being mentioned here.

Another early reference in the Talmud speaks of five of Jesus' disciples
and recounts their standing before judges who make individual decisions
about each one, deciding that they should be executed. However, no actual deaths are recorded.[37] From this second portion we can ascertain
only (6) the fact that Jesus had some disciples and (7) that some among

the Jews felt that these men were also guilty of actions which warranted execution.

There are various other references to Jesus in the Talmud, although most are from later periods of formulation and are of questionable historical value. For instance, one reference indicates that Jesus was treated differently from others who led the people astray, for he was connected with royalty.[38] The first portion of this statement is very possibly an indication of the fact that Jesus was crucified instead of being stoned. The second part could be referring to Jesus being born of the lineage of David, or it could actually be a criticism of the Christian belief that Jesus was the Messiah. Another possible reference to Jesus states that he was either thirty-three or thirty-four years old when he died.[39] Many other allusions and possible connections could be mentioned, such as derision of the Christian doctrine of the virgin birth[40] and references to Mary, Jesus' mother,[41] but these depend on questions of identification of pseudonyms and other such issues.

Because of the questionable nature and dates of these latter Talmudic references, we will utilize only the two earlier passages from the Tannaitic period in our study. While the latter references are interesting and may reflect older traditions, we cannot be sure.

Toledoth Jesu. This anti-Christian document not only refers to Jesus, but gives an interesting account of what happened to Jesus' body after his death. It relates that his disciples planned to steal his body. However, a gardener named Juda discovered their plans and dug a new grave in his garden. Then he removed Jesus' body from Joseph's tomb and placed it in his own newly dug grave. The disciples came to the original tomb, found Jesus' body gone and proclaimed him risen. The Jewish leaders also proceeded to Joseph's tomb and found it empty. Juda then took them to his grave and dug up the body of Jesus. The Jewish leaders were greatly relieved and wanted to take the body. Juda replied that he would sell them the body of Jesus and did so for thirty pieces of silver. The Jewish priests then dragged Jesus' body through the streets of Jerusalem.[42]

It is true that the *Toledoth Jesu* was not compiled until the fifth century A.D., although it does reflect early Jewish tradition. Even though Jewish scholars scorn the reliability of this source,[43] the teaching that the disciples were the ones who removed the dead body of Jesus persisted in the early centuries after Jesus' death. As reported in Matt. 28:11-15, this saying was still popular when the gospel was written, probably between 70-85 A.D. Additionally, Justin Martyr, writing about 150 A.D., states that

99

the Jewish leaders had even sent specially trained men around the Mediterranean, even to Rome, to further this teaching,[44] which is confirmed by Tertullian about 200 A.D.[45] In other words, even if the *Toledoth Jesu* itself is too late or untrustworthy as a source, in spite of its early material, the idea that the tomb was empty because the body was moved or stolen was common in early church history, as witnessed by other sources.

D. Other Gentile sources

Lucian. A second century Greek satirist, Lucian spoke rather derisively of Jesus and early Christians. His point was to criticize Christians for being such gullible people that, with very little warrant, they would approve charletons who pose as teachers, thereby supporting these persons even to the point of making them wealthy. In the process of his critique he relates some important facts concerning Jesus and Christians:

> The Christians, you know, worship a *man* to this day—the distinguished personage who introduced their novel rites, and was crucified on that account....You see, these misguided creatures start with the general conviction that they are immortal for all time, which explains the contempt of death and voluntary self-devotion which are so common among them; and then it was impressed on them by their original lawgiver that they are all brothers, from the moment that they are converted, and deny the gods of Greece, and worship the crucified sage, and live after his laws. All this they take quite on faith, with the result that they despise all worldly goods alike, regarding them merely as common property.[46]

From the material supplied by Lucian we may derive the following data concerning Jesus and early Christians. (1) We are told that Jesus was worshipped by Christians. (2) It is also related that Jesus introduced new teachings in Palestine (the location is given in another unquoted portion of Section II) and (3) that he was crucified because of these teachings. Jesus taught his followers certain doctrines, such as (4) all believers are brothers, (5) from the moment that conversion takes place and (6) after the false gods are denied (such as those of Greece). Additionally, these teachings included (7) worshipping Jesus and (8) living according to his laws. (9) Lucian refers to Jesus as a "sage," which, especially in a Greek context, would be to compare him to the Greek philosophers and wise men.

Concerning Christians, we are told (10) that they are followers of Jesus who (11) believe themselves to be immortal. Lucian explains that this latter belief accounts for their contempt of death. (12) Christians accepted Jesus' teachings by faith and (13) practiced their faith by their disregard for material possessions, as revealed by the holding of common property among believers.

The portion of Lucian not quoted presents some additional facts. (14) The Christians had "sacred writings" which were frequently read. (15) When something affected their community, "they spare no trouble, no expense." (16) However, Lucian notes that Christians were easily taken advantage of by unscrupulous individuals.[47] From Lucian, then, we learn a number of important facts about Jesus and early Christian beliefs. Many of these are not reported by other extra-New Testament authors.

Mara Bar-Serapion. The British Museum owns the manuscript of a letter written sometime between the late first and third centuries A.D. Its author was a Syrian named Mara Bar-Serapion, who was writing from prison to motivate his son Serapion to emulate wise teachers of the past:[48]

> What advantage did the Athenians gain from putting Socrates to death? Famine and plague came upon them as a judgment for their crime. What advantage did the men of Samos gain from burning Pythagoras? In a moment their land was covered with sand. What advantage did the Jews gain from executing their wise King? It was just after that that their kingdom was abolished. God justly avenged these three wise men: the Athenians died of hunger; the Samians were overwhelmed by the sea; the Jews, ruined and driven from their land, live in complete dispersion. But Socrates did not die for good; he lived on in the teaching of Plato. Pythagoras did not die for good; he lived on in the statue of Hera. Nor did the wise King die for good; he lived on in the teaching which he had given.[49]

From this passage we learn (1) that Jesus was considered to be a wise and virtuous man. (2) He is addressed twice as the Jews' King, possibly a reference to Jesus' own teachings about himself, to that of his followers or even to the wording on the *titulus* placed above Jesus' head on the cross. (3) Jesus was executed unjustly by the Jews, who paid for their misdeeds by suffering judgment soon afterward, probably at least a reference to the fall of Jerusalem to the Roman armies. (4) Jesus lived on in the teachings of the early Christians, which is an indication that Mara Bar-Serapion was almost certainly not a Christian. Rather, he follows Lucian and others in the popular comparison of Jesus to philosophers and other wise men of the ancient world.

As Bruce notes, some of Mara Bar-Serapion's material concerning Athens and Samos is quite inaccurate.[50] Yet the statements about Jesus do not appear to be flawed and thus add to our extra-New Testament data about him.

E. Gnostic sources

This category of extra-New Testament sources is different from all the others in that these works often at least make the claim to be Christian. Although scholars still debate the question of the origin of gnosticism, it is generally said to have flourished mainly from the second to the fourth centuries A.D. It is from four, second century documents that we get the material for this section. While it is certainly possible that there are other gnostic sources as old or older than the four used here, these have the advantage both of being better established and of claiming to relate facts concerning the historical Jesus, many of which are not reported in the Gospels.

However, it must be admitted that this group of writers was still more influenced by the New Testament writings than the others in this chapter. Yet, although many of the ideas in these four books are Christian, gnosticism in many of its forms and teachings was pronounced heretical and viewed as such by the church. Hence we are discussing such material in this chapter.

The Gospel of Truth. This book was very possibly written by the gnostic teacher Valentinus, which would date its writing around 135-160 A.D. If not, it was probably at least from this school of thought and still dated in the second century A.D.[51] Unlike some gnostic works, *The Gospel of Truth* addresses the subject of the historicity of Jesus in several short passages. It does not hesitate to affirm that the Son of God came in the flesh. The author asserts that "the Word came into the midst....it became a body."[52] Later he states:

> For when they had seen him and had heard him, he granted them to taste him and to smell him and to touch the beloved Son. When he had appeared instructing them about the Father....For he came by means of fleshly appearance.[53]

From these two quotations this book indicates (1) that Jesus was the Son of God, the Word and (2) that he became a man and took on an actual human body which could be perceived by all five senses. (3) We are also told that he instructed his listeners about his Father.

According to *The Gospel of Truth*, Jesus also died and was raised from the dead:

> Jesus was patient in accepting sufferings...since he knows that his death is life for many....he was nailed to a tree; he published the edict of the Father on the cross....He draws himself down to death through life. ...eternal clothes him. Having stripped himself of the perishable rags, he put on imperishability, which no one can possibly take away from him.[54]

Here and earlier (18:23) the author states (4) that Jesus was persecuted and suffered and (5) that he was "nailed to a tree," obviously referring to his crucifixion. (6) We are also told of the belief that it was Jesus' death that brought salvation "for many," which is referred to as the imparting of Light to those who would receive it (30:37; 31:12-20). It is also asserted (7) that Jesus was raised in an eternal body which no one can harm or take from him.

The theological overtones in *The Gospel of Truth* (as well as in other gnostic writings) present an obvious contrast to the ancient secular works inspected above. Yet, even allowing for such theological motivation, these early gnostic sources still present us with some important insights into the historical life and teachings of Jesus.

The Apocryphon of John. Grant asserts that this work is closely related to the thought of the gnostic teacher Saturninus, who taught around 120-130 A.D.[55] *The Apocryphon of John* was modified as it was passed on and was known in several versions. Irenaeus made use of one of these versions as a source for his treatment of gnosticism, *Against Heresies*, written ca. 185 A.D. Thus, by this time, at least the major teachings of *The Apocryphon of John* were in existence.[56]

In a largely mythical treatise involving esoteric matters of gnostic theology, this book does purport to open with a historical incident. We are told:

> It happened [one day] when Jo[hn, the brother] of James,—who are the sons of Ze[bed]ee—went up and came to the temple, that a [Ph]arisee named Arimanius approached him and said to him, "[Where] is your master whom you followed?" And he [said] to him, "He has gone to the place from which he came." The Pharisee said to him, "[This Nazarene]

deceived you (pl.) with deception and filled [your ears with lies] and closed [your hearts and turned you] from the traditions [of your fathers]."[57]

This passage relates (1) that John the disciple, in response to a question from Arimanius the Pharisee, stated that Jesus had returned to heaven, a possible reference to the Ascension. (2) The Pharisee responded by telling John that Jesus had deceived his followers with his teachings, which is reminiscent of the Talmud's statements about Jesus. Whether such an encounter between John and Arimanius actually occurred or not, such is apparently a typical view of Jesus' teachings from the standpoint of the Jewish leaders.

The Gospel of Thomas. This book describes itself in the opening statement as "the secret sayings which the living Jesus spoke."[58] Grant notes that this collection of teachings thereby purports to be the words of the risen Jesus, thus accounting for the almost complete absence of statements concerning his birth, life and death.[59]

The text is usually dated from around 140-200 A.D., although it reflects thought of even earlier periods.[60] As such it could present some accurate facts concerning Jesus.

In an incident very similar to Jesus' question at Caesarea Philippi,[61] reported in the synoptic Gospels, *The Gospel of Thomas* also presents Jesus asking his disciples, "Compare me to someone and tell Me whom I am like." They respond by describing him as an angel, a philosopher and as an indescribable personage.[62] In a later passage the disciples refer to Jesus as the consummation of the prophets (42:13-18).

Jesus is said to have partially answered his own question on several occasions. He describes himself as the Son of Man (47:34—48:4), which is also the name most commonly reported in the Gospels. On other occasions he speaks of himself in much more lofty terms. To Salome, Jesus states "I am He who exists from the Undivided. I was given some of the things of My father."[63] Elsewhere he speaks of himself as the Son in *The Gospel of Thomas.*[64] In another instance Jesus speaks in more specifically gnostic terminology:

Jesus said, "It is I who am the light which is above them all. It is I who am the All. From Me did the All come forth, and unto Me did the All extend. Split a piece of wood, and I am there. Lift up the stone, and you will find Me there.[65]

In these passages which concern the identity of Jesus, we are told (1) that Jesus asked his disciples for their view. (2) Their responses were varied, with the comparison of Jesus to a philosopher being especially reminiscent of the references by Lucian and Mara Bar-Serapion. Jesus then identified himself as (3) the Son of Man, (4) the Son of His Father and (5) as the All of the Universe.

The Gospel of Thomas also records a parable concerning the death of Jesus (45:1-16) and relates his subsequent exaltation (45:17-19). Again, Jesus is identified as "living" or as the "Living One," a reference to his post-resurrection life (see Rev. 1:17-18).[66] These references relate (6) the death of Jesus and (7) his exaltation as a result of his resurrection from the dead.

The foregoing references in *The Gospel of Thomas* require further comment. Initially, they often appear to be dependent on gospel testimony, especially in the question of Jesus' identity and in the parable of the vineyard. Additionally, the overly obvious gnostic tendencies, such as those found in the identification of Jesus with the "Undivided" and with the "All," including monistic tendencies, certainly cast doubt on the reliability of these reports.[67]

The Treatise On Resurrection. This book is addressed to an individual named Rheginos by an unknown author. Some have postulated that Valentinus is the author, but most scholars object to this hypothesis. The ideas are somewhat Valentinian, which could point to the presence of earlier ideas, but it is probably better to date the work itself from the late second century A.D.[68]

For the author of *The Treatise of the Resurrection*, Jesus became a human being but was still divine:

> The Lord...existed in flesh and...revealed himself as Son of God...Now the Son of God, Rheginos, was Son of Man. He embraced them both, possessing the humanity and the divinity, so that on the one hand he might vanquish death through his being Son of God, and that on the other through the Son of Man the restoration to the Pleroma might occur; because he was originally from above, a seed of the Truth, before this structure (of the cosmos) had come into being.[69]

In this passage we find much gnostic terminology in addition to the teachings (1) that Jesus became flesh as the Son of Man in spite of (2) his true divinity as the Son of God who conquers death.

So Jesus came to this world in the flesh of a man, died and rose again:

> For we have known the Son of Man, and we have believed that he rose from among the dead. This is he of whom we say, "He became the destruction of death, as he is a great one in whom they believe." Great are those who believe.[70]

In less esoteric language we are told (3) that Jesus died, (4) rose again and (5) thereby destroyed death for those who believe in him.

We are told of Jesus' resurrection in other passages as well:

> The Savior swallowed up death....He transformed [himself] into an imperishable Aeon and raised himself up, having swallowed the visible by the invisible, and he gave us the way of our immortality.[71]

> Do not think the resurrection is an illusion. It is no illusion, but it is truth. Indeed, it is more fitting to say that the world is an illusion, rather than the resurrection which has come into being through our Lord the Savior, Jesus Christ.[72]

These two quotations even present an interesting contrast on the subjects of Jesus' death and resurrection. While the first statement is mixed with gnostic terminology, the second assures believers that the resurrection was not an illusion, which reminds us of some gnostic tendencies to deny the actual, physical death of Christ.[73]

Since Jesus has been raised the author counsels Rheginos that "already you have the resurrection...why not consider yourself as risen and (already) brought to this?" Thus he is encouraged not to "continue as if you are to die."[74] The resurrection of Jesus thereby provides practical considerations in causing the believer to realize that he already has eternal life presently and should not live in fear of death. This teaching is similar to that of the New Testament (Col. 3:1-4; Heb. 2:14-15) and gives added significance to Lucian's report of Christians who believe that they are immortal and thus unafraid of death.

Once again, these previous four sources are theologically oriented, freely incorporating many gnostic tendencies, in addition to being generally later than most of our other sources. While these two qualifications do not necessitate unreliable reporting of historical facts about Jesus, we are to be cautious in our use of this data.

F. Other lost works

Acts of Pontius Pilate. The contents of this purportedly lost document are reported by both Justin Martyr (ca. 150 A.D.) and Tertullian (ca. 200 A.D.). Both agree that it was an official document of Rome. Two types of archives were kept in ancient Rome. The *Acta senatus* were composed of minutes of the senatorial meetings. These contained no discussions of Christ or Christianity as far as is known. The *Commentarii principis* were composed of the correspondence sent to the emperors from various parts of the empire. Any report from Pilate to Tiberius would belong to this second group.[75]

Justin Martyr reported around 150 A.D. in his *First Apology* that the details of Jesus' crucifixion could be validated from Pilate's report:

> And the expression, 'They pierced my hands and my feet,' was used in reference to the nails of the cross which were fixed in His hands and feet. And after he was crucified, they cast lots upon his vesture, and they that crucified Him parted it among them. And that these things did happen you can ascertain the 'Acts' of Pontius Pilate.[76]

Later in the same work Justin lists several healing miracles and asserts, "And that He did those things, you can learn from the Acts of Pontius Pilate."[77]

Justin Martyr relates several facts, believing them to be contained in Pilate's report. The chief concern is apparently Jesus' crucifixion, with details such as (1) his hands and feet being nailed to the cross and (2) the soldiers gambling for his garments. But it is also asserted (3) that several of Jesus' miracles were also included in Pilate's report.

Tertullian even reports that Tiberius acted on the report:

> Tiberius accordingly, in whose days the Christian name made its entry into the world, having himself received intelligence from Palestine of events which had clearly shown the truth of Christ's divinity, brought the matter before the senate, with his own decision in favour of Christ. The senate, because it had not given the approval itself, rejected his proposal. Caesar held to his opinion, threatening wrath against all accusers of the Christians[78]

Tertullian's account claims (4) that Tiberius actually brought details of Christ's life before the Roman Senate, apparently for a vote of approval. The Senate then reportedly spurned Tiberius' own vote of approval, which engendered a warning from the emperor not to attempt actions against Christians. As noted by Bruce, this incident, which Tertullian apparently accepts as accurate, is quite an improbable occurrence. It is difficult to accept such an account when the work reporting it is about 170 years later than the event, with seemingly no good intervening sources for such acceptance.[79]

It should be noted that the *Acts of Pilate* referred to here should not be confused with later fabrications by the same name, which may certainly have been written to take the place of these records which were believed to exist.

There may well have been an original report sent from Pilate to Tiberius, containing some details of Jesus' crucifixion. In spite of this, it is questionable if Justin Martyr and Tertullian knew what any possible report contained. Although the early Christian writers had reason to believe such a document existed, evidence such as that found in the reference to Thallus is missing here. In particular, there are no known fragments of the *Acts of Pilate* or any evidence that it was specifically quoted by another writer. Additionally, it is entirely possible that what Justin thought original was actually a concurrent apocryphal gospel.[80] At any rate, we cannot be positive as to this purported imperial document. Like the gnostic sources, we therefore are cautious in our use of this source.

Phlegon. The last reference to be discussed in this chapter is that of Phlegon, whom Anderson describes as "a freedman of the Emperor Hadrian who was born about A.D. 80." Origen relates that Phlegon mentioned that Jesus made certain predictions which had been fulfilled.[81] This work of Phlegon is no longer in existence and we depend on Origen for this information. This source reports that Jesus did successfully predict certain future events.

G. Synopsis: Jesus and ancient Christianity

When the combined evidence from ancient secular sources is summarized, quite an impressive amount of information is gathered concerning Jesus and ancient Christianity. It is our purpose in this section to make a brief composite picture of the historical data. We have investigated a total of seventeen sources that present valuable material with regard to the historical Jesus and early Christianity. As noted above, not all of these records are equally good documents, but even minus the questionable sources, this early evidence is still very impressive.[82] Few ancient historical figures can boast the same amount of material.

The Life and Person of Jesus. According to the sources which we have investigated above, the ministry of Jesus, the brother of James (Josephus), was geographically centered in Palestine (Tacitus, Lucian, Acts of Pilate). Jesus was known as a wise, virtuous and ethical man (Josephus, Mara Bar-Serapion), who was reported to have both performed miracles (Acts of Pilate) and made prophecies which were later fulfilled (Phlegon, cf. Josephus). A result of his ministry was that he had many disciples, from both the Jews and the Gentiles (Josephus, Talmud).

Of the sources which we studied, the gnostic works, in particular, comment on the person of Jesus. They relate that on one occasion he asked his disciples who they thought he was (Gospel of Thomas). Although there were varied answers to his question, these works agree that Jesus was both God and man. While he was a flesh and blood person (Gospel of Truth, Treatise on Resurrection), as indicated by the title "Son of Man" (Gospel of Thomas), he is also said to be the Son of God (Treatise on Resurrection, Gospel of Truth, Gospel of Thomas), the Word (Gospel of Truth) and the "All" (Gospel of Thomas).

As pointed out earlier these gnostic works are somewhat questionable sources for the historical Jesus because of their late and theological character. However, some secular sources for the historical Jesus report similar beliefs. They assert that Jesus was worshipped as deity (Pliny, Lucian), and that some believed he was the Messiah (Josephus) and even call him "King" (Mara Bar-Serapion). At least these beliefs on the part of certain persons are a matter of historical record.

The Teachings of Jesus. An interesting tendency among some ancient authors was to view Jesus as a philosopher with some distinctive teachings (Lucian, Mara Bar-Serapion, cf. Gospel of Thomas). Lucian lists some of Jesus' teachings as the need for conversion, the importance of faith and obedience, the brotherhood of all believers, the requirements of abandoning the gods of other systems of belief and the worship of himself, which was either taught or at least the result of his teaching. It might also be inferred that the Christian belief in immortality and lack of fear of death reported by Lucian is also due to Jesus' teaching.

Pliny's report that believers took oaths not to commit unrighteousness is probably also due to Jesus' warnings against sin. The *Gospel of Truth* adds that Jesus taught his listeners about his Father and that Jesus realized that his death was the means of life for many.

The Death of Jesus. The Jewish leaders judged that Jesus was guilty of teaching spiritual apostasy, thereby leading Israel astray (Talmud, cf. Apocryphon of John). So the Jews sent a herald proclaiming that Jesus would be stoned for his false teaching and invited anyone who wished to defend him to do so. But none came forth to support him (Talmud).

After suffering persecution (Gospel of Truth) and as a result of his teachings (Lucian), Jesus was put to death (Gospel of Thomas, Treatise on Resurrection). He died at the hands of Roman procurator Pontius Pilate (Tacitus), who crucified him (Josephus, Talmud, Lucian, Gospel of Truth, Acts of Pilate) during the reign of Emperor Tiberius (Tacitus). Even some details of the crucifixion are provided. The event occurred on Passover Eve (Talmud) and included being nailed to a cross (Gospel of Truth, Acts of Pilate, cf. Tacitus), after which his executioners gambled for his garments (Acts of Pilate). One writer (Mara Bar-Serapion) asserted that Jesus was executed unjustly and that the Jews were judged accordingly by God.

The Resurrection of Jesus. After Jesus' death it is recorded that his teachings broke out again in Judea (Tacitus, cf. Suetonius, Pliny). What was the cause for this new activity and spread of Jesus' teachings after his death? Could Jesus have been raised from the dead? Various answers are mentioned.

According to the *Toledoth Jesu*, the disciples were going to steal the body, so Juda the gardener reburied it and later sold the body of Jesus to the Jewish leaders, who dragged it down the streets of Jerusalem. Justin Martyr and Tertullian object, asserting that the Jews sent trained men around the Mediterranean region in order to say that the disciples stole the body. The earliest of the sources, Matt. 28:11-15, claims that after Jesus was raised from the dead, the Jewish leaders bribed the guards in order to have them say that the disciples stole the body, even though they did not.

Mar Bar-Serapion points out that Jesus' teachings lived on in his disciples. Josephus records the disciples' belief in the resurrection of Jesus, noting that these witnesses claimed to have seen Jesus alive three days after his crucifixion. The resurrection of Jesus is defended especially by *The Treatise on Resurrection*, but also proclaimed by *The Gospel of Truth* and *The Gospel of Thomas*. Afterward, Jesus was exalted (Apocryphon of John, Gospel of Thomas).

Christian Teachings and Worship. Christians were named after their founder, Christ (Tacitus), whose teachings they followed (Lucian). Believers were of all classes, ages, localities and of both sexes, forming a cross section of society (Pliny). For Christians, Jesus' death procured salvation (Gospel of Truth) for those who exercised faith in his teachings (Lucian). As a result, Christians believed in their own immortality and scorned death (Lucian), realizing that eternal life was a present possession (Treatise on Resurrection).

Additionally, Lucian relates several other Christian teachings. Believers had sacred writings which were frequently read. They practiced their faith by denying material goods and by holding common property. They went to any extent to help with matters pertaining to their community. However, Lucian does complain that Christians were gullible enough to be taken advantage of by unscrupulous persons.

Pliny relates that believers met in a pre-dawn service on a certain day (probably Sunday). There they sang verses of a hymn, worshipped Christ as deity and made oaths against committing sin. Then they would disband, only to reassemble in order to share food together, which is very probably a reference to the love feast and Lord's supper. Pliny also makes reference to the existence of positions in the early church when he mentions two female deaconesses.

The Spread of Christianity and Persecution. After the death of Jesus and the reported resurrection appearances, the disciples did not abandon the teachings which they learned from him (Josephus). By the middle of the first century, Christian doctrine, and the crucifixion of Jesus in particular, had spread around the Mediterranean. In fact, skeptics were already offering rationalistic explanations for supernatural claims only some twenty years after Jesus' death (Thallus).

More specifically, Christian teachings had reached Rome by 49 A.D., less than twenty years after the death of Jesus, when Claudius expelled Jews from the city because of what was thought to be the influence of Jesus' teachings (Suetonius). By the time of Nero's reign (54-68 A.D.), Christians were still living in Rome (Tacitus, Suetonius). We are also told that Christians were present during the fall of Jerusalem in 70 A.D. (Tacitus).

The spread of Christianity unfortunately involved persecution fairly early in its history. Sometimes it was tempered by a certain amount of fairness, but it was real and serious for many early believers, nonetheless. The Talmud relates an occasion when five of Jesus' disciples were judged to be worthy of death. Tacitus provides much greater detail. After the great fire at Rome, Nero blamed the occurrence on Christians, who are

111

described as a group of people who were hated by the Roman populace. As a result, many believers were arrested, convicted, mocked and finally tortured to death. Being nailed to crosses and being burnt to death are two methods which are specifically mentioned. Such treatment evoked compassion from the people, and Tacitus blamed these events on the eccentricities of Nero.

Christians were sometimes reported as lawbreakers (Pliny, cf. Trajan, Hadrian) for almost three centuries after the death of Jesus, after which Christianity became the official religion of the Roman Empire. Believers were blamed with meeting secretly, burning their children and drinking blood.

For instance, Pliny's letter relates his methodology with Bithynian Christians. They were identified, interrogated, sometimes tortured and then executed. If they denied that they were believers, as demonstrated by their worshipping Caesar and the gods, they were freed. Pliny noted that true believers would never be guilty of such a denial of Christ.

Trajan's response encouraged moderation. Repentance and worship of the gods were sufficient for freeing these people. But they should not be sought out. Hadrian offered similar advice prohibiting the harassment of Christians and even ordered that their enemies be dealt with if they acted improperly against believers. However, if Christians were guilty, they would have to be punished.

H. Conclusion

This chapter has shown that ancient extra-biblical sources do present a surprisingly large amount of detail concerning both the life of Jesus and the nature of early Christianity. While many of these facts are quite well known, we must remember that they have been documented here apart from the usage of the New Testament. When viewed in that light, we should realize that it is quite extraordinary that we could provide a broad outline of most of the major facts of Jesus' life from "secular" history alone. Such is surely significant.

Using only the information gleaned from these ancient extra-biblical sources, what can we conclude concerning the death and resurrection of Jesus? Can these events be historically established based on these sources alone? Of the seventeen documents examined in this chapter, eleven different works speak of the death of Jesus in varying amounts of detail, with five of these specifying crucifixion as the mode. When these sources are examined by normal historical procedures used with other ancient documents, the result is conclusive.[83] It is this author's view that the death of Jesus by crucifixion can be asserted as a historical fact from this data. This conclusion is strengthened by the variety of details which are related by good sources. As mentioned often, a few of the documents may be contested, but the entire bulk of evidence points quite probably to the historicity of Jesus' death due to the rigors of crucifixion.

The ancient references to the resurrection are fewer and more questionable. Of the seventeen sources, only six either imply or report this occurrence, with four of these works being questioned in our study. Before answering the issue concerning Jesus' resurrection, we will initially address the cognate point of whether the empty tomb can be established as historical by this extra-biblical evidence alone. There are some strong considerations in its favor.

First, the Jewish sources which we have examined admit the empty tomb, thereby providing evidence from hostile documents. Josephus notes the disciples' belief in Jesus' resurrection, while the *Toledoth Jesu* specifically acknowledges the empty tomb. Justin Martyr and Tertullian confirm Matt. 28:11-15 by asserting that Jewish leaders were still admitting the empty tomb over a century later. While these Jewish sources (with exception of Josephus) teach that the body was stolen or moved, they still admit the empty tomb.

Second, there are apparently no ancient sources which assert that the tomb still contained Jesus' body. While such an argument from silence does not prove anything, it is made stronger by the first consideration from the hostile sources and further complements it.

Third, our study has shown that Jesus taught in Palestine and was crucified and buried in Jerusalem under Pontius Pilate. These sources assert that Christianity had its beginnings in the same location. But could Christianity have survived in this location, based on its central claim that Jesus was raised from the dead, if the tomb had not been empty?

It must be remembered that the resurrection of the body was the predominent view of first century Jews. To declare a bodily resurrection if the body was still in a nearby tomb points out the dilemma here. Of all places, evidence was readily available in Jerusalem to disprove this central tenet of Christian belief. The Jewish leaders had both a motive and the means to get such evidence if it were available. As expressed by historian of antiquity, Paul Maier, speaking of the birth of Christianity:

113

But this is the very *last* place it could have started if Jesus' tomb had remained occupied, since anyone producing a dead Jesus would have driven a wooden stake through the heart of an incipient Christianity inflamed by his supposed resurrection.[84]

Based on the evidence admitted by hostile documents, the absence of contrary data and the important information concerning the location of the message, we conclude that there is some probability for the empty tomb based on ancient extra-biblical sources alone. Maier confirms this:

> Accordingly, if all the evidence is weighed carefully and fairly, it is indeed justifiable, according to the canons of historical research, to conclude that the sepulcher of Joseph of Arimathea, in which Jesus was buried, was actually empty on the morning of the first Easter.[85]

Dealing with different factual data, Michael Grant agrees from a historical viewpoint:

> But if we apply the same sort of criteria that we would apply to any other ancient literary sources, then the evidence is firm and plausible enough to necessitate the conclusion that the tomb was indeed found empty.[86]

But what about the teaching that the disciples or someone else stole the dead body of Jesus? Does this account for the empty tomb and end the question of Jesus' resurrection?

Contemporary critical scholars, whether skeptical or not, are virtually unanimous in rejecting such hypotheses.[87] If the disciples stole the body, they would not have willingly died, in all probability, for a known lie or fraud.[88] Liars do not make good martyrs. Additionally, the changed lives of the earliest disciples and their belief that Jesus was raised, both of which are admitted by critics, are unexplained if they stole the body. These and several other considerations such as the quality of ethical teachings of the disciples account for the dismissal of this view even by critical scholars. As far as this author knows, it has not been held by a reputable scholar for over 200 years.[89]

Equally faulty is the hypothesis that the body of Jesus was taken or moved by someone other than the disciples. The major problem, among others, is that it does not account for the strongest, critically ascertained fact in favor of the resurrection—the disciples' belief that the risen Jesus had literally appeared to them. Since one must search elsewhere to account for this major fact, this view cannot disprove the resurrection. Additionally, such views fail to provide a plausible person(s) to perform such an act, viable motives, a place for Jesus' final burial, or for the fact that the act was never admitted, discovered or otherwise reported. But again, the appearances of Jesus are not even dealt with by these theses, and this constitutes the primary refutation. Also, it should be remembered that the *Toledoth Jesu*, which purports the view that Jesus' body was dragged down Jerusalem's streets, is a much later source, and is disdained as nonhistorical even by most Jewish scholars. Its thesis fails because such an act would have killed Christianity centuries ago, when such an act obviously did not occur. Neither does it explain Jesus' appearances. It is no wonder that these fraud hypotheses have also had no reputable supporters in the last two centuries.[90]

However, we still cannot conclude that ancient extra-biblical sources historically demonstrate the resurrection, as is true with Jesus' death by crucifixion. The evidence indicates that alternative theories involving a stolen or moved body are invalid, and that the empty tomb is probable, but the cause of this event cannot be proven at this point. We conclude that ancient extra-biblical sources both provide a broad outline of the life of Jesus and indicate that he died due to the effects of crucifixion. Afterwards he was buried and his tomb was later found empty, but the body had not been stolen or moved. While we have this mystery and some factual evidence in favor of Jesus' resurrection, we must await a further examination of the data in order to reach a final position.

Notes

[1]Hadas, "Introduction" to *Tacitus*, IX, XIII-XIX.

[2]An alternate theory is that the *Annals* included sixteen books and the *Histories*, fourteen books, also for a total of thirty (cf. Hadas, p. XII).

[3]*Tacitus*, 15.44.

[4]Ibid.

[5]F. F. Bruce, *Jesus and Christian Origins Outside the New Testament* (Grand Rapids: William B. Eerdman's Publishing Company, 1974), p. 23. This book will hereafter be referred to as *Christian Origins*.

[6]J. N. D. Anderson, *Christianity: The Witness of History* (London: Tyndale Press, 1969), p. 19.

[7]*Chronicles* 2:30.6.

[8]Robert Graves, "Introduction" to Suetonius' *The Twelve Caesars*, transl. by Robert Graves (Baltimore: Penguin Books, 1957), p. 7.

[9]Amiot, "Jesus A Historical Person," p. 8.

[10]Suetonius, *Claudius*, 25.

[11]Graves, p. 197; Bruce, *Christian Origins*, p. 21; Amiot, p. 8.

[12]Suetonius, *Nero*, 16.

[13]Daniel-Rops, "Silence of Jesus' Contemporaries," pp. 19-21; Bruce *The New Testament Documents*, pp. 102-103.

[14]*Antiquities*, 20:9. The edition of Josephus used here is *The Works of Josephus*, transl. by William Wiston (Philadelphia: David McKay Publishers, n.d.).

[15]*Antiquities*, 18:3.

[16]*Contra Celsum* 1:47.

[17]*Ecclesiastical History*, 1:XI.

[18]Daniel-Rops, "Silence of Jesus' Contemporaries," p. 21.

[19]Ibid.; Anderson, p. 20; Bruce, *The New Testament Documents*, p. 108. Cf. also Bruce, p. 109 for the views of British authority H. St. John Thackery and Jewish scholar Joseph Klausner.

[20]*Antiquities*, 18:3 as it appears in the Arabic text as initially printed in "New Evidence on Jesus' Life Reported" and "Two Views of Jesus," *The New York Times*, February 12, 1972, pp. 1, 24. See also Maier, *First Easter*, p. 116.

[21]"New Evidence on Jesus' Life Reported."

[22]Bruce presents a somewhat similar list of facts. See *The New Testament Documents*, p. 112.

[23]Bruce, *Christian Origins*, pp. 29-30.

[24]Ibid.; Anderson, *Witness of History*, p. 19.

[25]Bruce, *The New Testament Documents*, p. 113.

[26]See the discussion below on the Talmud (*Sanhedrin* 43a).

[27]Bruce, *Christian Origins*, p. 24.

[28]*Letters*, X: 96, transl. by William Melmoth (Cambridge: Harvard University Press, 1935), vol. II.

[29]Ibid.

[30]Ibid.

[31]Ibid., X: 97.

[32]Eusebius, *Ecclesiastical History*, IV: IX, transl. by Christian Frederick Cruse (Grand Rapids: Baker Book House, 1969).

[33]Ibid.

[34]Bruce, *Christian Origins*, pp. 54-55.

[35]This quotation was taken from the reading in *The Babylonian Talmud*, transl. by I. Epstein (London: The Soncino Press, 1935), vol. III, *Sanhedrin* 43a, p. 281.

[36]Greek *stauros*, as in such references as Matt. 27:31; Mark 15:13, 14, 20, 27, etc.

[37]*Sanhedrin* 43a.

[38]*Sanhedrin* 43a, where this reference is apparently a third century addition to

the earlier material in this section of the Talmud.

[39]*Sanhedrin* 106b.

[40]For instance, *Yeb.* IV: 3, 49a.

[41]*Hagigah* 4b; *Sanhedrin* 106a.

[42]Maier, *First Easter*, pp. 117-118.

[43]Ibid., pp. 118-119.

[44]Justin Martyr, *Dialogue with Trypho*, 108.

[45]Tertullian, *On Spectacles*, 30.

[46]Lucian, *The Death of Peregrine*, 11-13, in *The Works of Lucian of Samosata*, transl. by H. W. Fowler and F. G. Fowler, 4 vols. (Oxford: The Clarendon Press, 1949), vol. 4.

[47]These additional facts are found in Lucian, ibid., 12-13.

[48]Bruce, *Christian Origins*, p. 30.

[49]British Museum, Syriac Manuscript, Additional 14,658. For this text, see Bruce, *Christian Origins*, p. 31.

[50]Bruce, p. 31.

[51]For scholarly views on this question of authorship, see Hans Jonas, *The Gnostic Religion* (Boston: Beacon Press, 1963), p. 40; Robert M. Grant, *Gnosticism and Early Christianity*, revised edition (New York: Harper and Row, Publishers, 1966), pp. 5, 128-134; George W. MacRae, "Introduction," *The Gospel of Truth* in James M. Robinson, editor, *The Nag Hammadi Library* (New York: Harper and Row, Publishers, 1981), p. 37.

[52]*The Gospel of Truth*, 26:4-8. The edition used here is Robinson, ibid.

[53]Ibid., 30:27-33; 31:4-6.

[54]Ibid., 20:11-14, 25-34.

[55]Grant, *Gnosticism and Early Christianity*, p. 109.

[56]Ibid., pp. 109-112; Jonas, *Gnostic Religion* 40, 199-205; Frederik Wisse, "Introduction" in James Robinson, *The Nag Hammadi Library*, p. 98; Walter Baur, *Orthodoxy and Heresy in Earliest Christianity*, ed. by Robert Kraft and Gerhard Krodel (Philadelphia: Fortress Press, 1971), p. 49.

[57]*The Apocryphon of John*, 1:5-17.

[58]*The Gospel of Thomas*, 32:10-11.

[59]See Grant, *Gnosticism and Early Christianity*, pp. 183-184.

[60]Helmut Koester, "Introduction" in James Robinson, *The Nag Hammadi Library*, p. 117; Baur, p. 310; Pagels, *Gnostic Gospels*, XV-XVI.

[61]Mark 8:27-30; Matt. 16:13-17; Luke 9:18-21.

[62]*The Gospel of Thomas*, 34:30—35:4.

[63]Ibid., 43:82-30.

[64]Ibid., 44:34-35; 45:11-15; 49:21-26.

[65]Ibid., 46:23-28.

[66]Ibid., 32:10-11; 43:9-12; cf. 42:13-36.

[67]See Chapter III, Section E, where such gnostic tendencies are evaluated in comparison to the canonical Gospels.

[68]Malcolm L. Peel, "Introduction" in James Robinson, *The Nag Hammadi Library*, p. 50.

[69]*The Treatise on Resurrection*, 44:13-36.

[70]Ibid., 46:14-21; cf. 44:27-29.

[71]Ibid., 45:14-23.

[72]Ibid., 48:10-19.

[73]For instance, see *The Second Treatise of the Great Seth*, 55:9—56:19.

[74]*The Treatise on Resurrection*, 49:15-27.

[75]Daniel-Rops, "Silence of Jesus' Contemporaries," p. 14.

[76]Justin Martyr, *First Apology*, XXXV. Quotations from Justin Martyr and Tertullian are from the *Ante-Nicene Fathers*, ed. by Alexander Roberts and James Donaldson (Grand Rapids: William B. Eerdmans Publishing Company, 1973), Vol. III.

[77]Justin Martyr, XLVIII.

[78]Tertullian, *Apology*, V.

[79]See Bruce, *New Testament Documents*, p. 116, for an analysis of Tertullian's statement.

[80]Daniel-Rops, p. 14.

[81]See J. N. D. Anderson, *Witness of History*, p. 19.

[82]Sources that have raised various kinds of doubt are the *Toledoth Jesu*, the four gnostic works and the *Acts of Pilate*, which make up approximately one-third of the total number of documents studied in this chapter.

[83]Cf. Michael Grant, *Jesus*, pp. 199-200.

[84]Paul L. Maier, "The Empty Tomb as History" in *Christianity Today*, 29/13, March 28, 1975, p. 5.

[85]Ibid., p. 6.

[86]Michael Grant, p. 176.

[87]See Chapter VI for a further treatment of these two theories and the critically attested historical facts which refute them.

[88]See Eusebius, I:IX; II:XXIII; II:XXV for accounts of the matyrdoms of several of the disciples.

[89]For example, see Schweitzer's *The Quest of the Historical Jesus*, who lists no proponent of this theory since 1778.

[90]On the contemporary rejection of these fraud theories, see Karl Barth, *Church Dogmatics*, vol. IV, p. 340; Raymond Brown, "The Resurrection and Biblical Criticism," p. 233.

5

Primary Sources: Creeds and Facts

What facts did the earliest Christians report concerning Jesus in the initial years after his crucifixion? Of what did the earliest Christology consist before the composition of the New Testament? Is it possible to get back to eyewitness testimony and to historical facts with regard to Jesus? These are fascinating and very important questions, and one of the chief efforts of contemporary scholarship has been to address these issues. Such is also a major concern in this book.

In this chapter we will endeavor to investigate an area which many feel is the most promising means of describing the nature of Christian thought before the writing of the New Testament. This general subject concerns the existence of early Christian creeds which were first repeated verbally and later written in the books of the New Testament. Thus, in one sense, this material is not extra-biblical since we rely on the scriptural material for the creeds. At the same time, this data was formulated *before* the New Testament books, in which the creeds appear, were actually written. In short, these creeds were communicated verbally years before they were written and hence they preserve some of the earliest reports concerning Jesus from about 30-50 A.D. Therefore, in a real sense, the creeds preserve pre-New Testament material, and are our earliest sources for the life of Jesus.

This chapter also includes a listing of facts which are admitted by virtually all critical scholars who study this subject. In other words, critical theologians, historians and philosophers who have studied the New Testament have ascertained a number of facts from the life of Jesus by the critical examination of the biblical sources. The procedure in this chapter is first to examine some Christological creeds with regard to the information they relate concerning the life, death and resurrection of Jesus. This last subject will be the special concern in the second section of this chapter, as we investigate 1 Cor. 15:3ff., which is perhaps the most important creed in the New Testament (at least for our purposes).

This is followed by the presentation of the critically accepted facts, as mentioned above. Lastly, an examination of this data will follow.

A. Christological creeds

In the early church there were multiple creedal formulas which corresponded to various circumstances in the Christian faith. The most common of these confessions were purely Christological in nature.[1] The two most common elements in these creeds concerned the death and resurrection of Jesus and his resulting deity.[2] Thus we note the major interest in the life and person of Jesus Christ.

The Life of Jesus. The earliest Christians were confident that "Jesus Christ is come in the flesh," as proclaimed in the confession found in 1 John 4:2.[3] Seldom was belief in Jesus' incarnation expressed more clearly than in the "pre-Pauline hymn" of Phil 2:6ff.,[4] which speaks of both Jesus' human and divine natures. His humble life on earth is clearly contrasted with his heavenly position "in the form of God" and his later exaltation and worship.

Another ancient creed which expresses a contrast between aspects of Jesus' life is 2 Tim. 2:8.[5] Here Jesus' birth in the lineage of David is contrasted with his resurrection from the dead, again showing the early Christian interest in linking Jesus to history.[6] Similarly, Rom. 1:3-4 is also an ancient, pre-Pauline creed.[7] It juxtaposes the man Jesus "made of the seed of David according to the flesh" with the divine Jesus whose claims were vindicated by his rising from the dead.[8] For our present purposes, we need only note the early interest in Jesus' earthly, physical connections, as he was born of a descendant of David's family. As Moule relates, it was the same human Jesus who lived, died and was later vindicated.[9]

One early confessional creed is 1 Tim. 3:16[10] (sometimes referred to as a "Christ-hymn"[11]), which gives a brief recital of both the human and divine Jesus:

Great indeed, we confess, is the mystery of our religion:

> He was manifested in the flesh,
> vindicated in the Spirit,
> seen by angels,
> preached among the nations,

believed on in the world,
taken up in glory. (RSV)

Moule notes not only the early date of this creed but also its pattern of rhyme, which was probably utilized in worship and hymnody.[12] This statement also presents a contrast between Jesus' human birth "in the flesh" and his deity,[13] further mentioning his approval by the Spirit and the witness of the angels. He was preached among the nations of the world and believed by people before he was "taken up in glory."

Another early confession which may well reflect an event in Christ's life is Rom. 10:9.[14] At present we are only concerned with the strong possibility that this may actually be a baptismal creed, cited by Christian candidates for baptism.[15] As such, it would be an indirect reference to Jesus' own baptism.

Although these early creeds are interested in theological elements of Christology, to be sure, they are also early reports of events in the life of Jesus. We are told (1) that Jesus was really born in human flesh (Phil. 2:6; 1 Tim. 3:16; 1 John 4:2) (2) of the lineage and family of David (Rom. 1:3-4; 2 Tim. 2:8). We find (3) an implication of his baptism (Rom. 10:9) and (4) that his word was preached, (5) resulting in persons believing his message (1 Tim. 3:16).

The Death and Resurrection of Jesus. Just prior to Jesus' trial and crucifixion, both the synoptic Gospels and Paul relate that Jesus had a private supper with his disciples. The Pauline account in 1 Cor. 11:23ff. presents a fixed tradition which is probably based on material independent of the sources for the synoptic Gospels.[16] Jeremias notes that Paul's words "received" and "delivered" are not Paul's typical terms, but "represent the rabbinical technical terms" for passing on tradition.[17] Additionally, there are other non-Pauline phrases such as "he was betrayed," "when he had given thanks" and "my body" (11:23-24), which are further indications of the early nature of this report. In fact, Jeremias asserts that his material was formulated "in the very earliest period; at any rate before Paul...a pre-Pauline formula." Paul is actually pointing out "that the chain of tradition goes back unbroken to Jesus himself."[18]

It is widely held that this ancient tradition presents actual historical events which occurred on the evening of the so-called "last supper."[19] Such is even recognized by Bultmann.[20] As Martin Hengel explains, "Paul refers to a historical event with a specific date..."[21] This tradition relates that Jesus did attend a dinner on the same evening as he was betrayed. He gave thanks to God before eating and afterward shared both bread and drink, which he referred to as the sacrifice of his body and blood for believers. Here we find insights not only to some of the events of the evening, but also to the actual words which may have been repeated at early Christian observances of the Last Supper.[22]

Another event just prior to Jesus' crucifixion is related by 1 Tim. 6:13, which is also an early tradition,[23] and perhaps even a part of a more extensive oral Christian confession of faith.[24] This statement asserts that Jesus came before Pontius Pilate and made a good confession.[25] Neufeld points out that Jesus' testimony was probably his affirmative answer to Pilate's question as to whether he was the King of the Jews (see Mark 15:2).[26] At any rate, "Jesus did not deny his identity in the trials but made a good confession before the Jews and Pilate."[27]

We have already noted how some early Christian traditions presented a juxtaposition between the human and the divine Jesus. Several other early reports contrasted the seeming defeat suffered at the Cross with the triumph of Jesus' resurrection. Earlier, Phil. 2:6ff. was mentioned as expressing this first comparison of the human Jesus who was to be exalted by God. More specifically, Phil. 2:8 additionally reports the humbling of Jesus as he died on the Cross in direct contrast to this later exaltation. Another example is found in Rom. 4:25, which Bultmann refers to as "a statement that had evidently existed before Paul and had been handed down to him."[28] The content of this tradition is that Jesus died for our sins and was afterward raised from the dead to secure the believer's justification. Similarly, 1 Pet. 3:18 (cf. 1 Tim. 2:6) also contrasts Jesus' death for the sins of mankind (in spite of his own righteousness) with the resurrection as the means of bringing people to God.[29]

Early accounts of Jesus' resurrection are also preserved in Christian tradition. Jeremias holds that Luke's brief mention of Jesus' resurrection appearance to Peter in Luke 24:34 is of even greater antiquity than is 1 Cor. 15:5, which would make this an extremely early witness to these appearances.[30] Dodd and Bultmann also note the connections between the fact that Peter appears in the references in both Luke 24:34 and 1 Cor. 15:5.[31] A previously mentioned tradition, 2 Tim. 2:8, presents another contrast by linking the Jesus who descended from David with the same person who was raised from the dead. Not only is Jesus' resurrection proclaimed as an event of history, but early creeds also assert that, on the basis of this event, Jesus' claims were justified. In particular, it is said that the resurrection revealed the uniqueness of Jesus' person.

That Rom. 1:3-4 is an ancient pre-Pauline creed is shown by the parallelism of the clauses,[32] which is especially seen in the contrast between Jesus as both the son of David and the Son of God.[33] The same Jesus who was born in space and time was raised from the dead.[34] This creed proclaims that Jesus was shown to be the Son of God, Christ (or Messiah) and Lord and vindicated as such by his resurrection from the dead.[35] Cullmann adds that redemption and Jesus' final exaltation were also included in this significant creedal affirmation.[36] Such an encompassing statement, including three major Christological titles and implying some of the actions of Jesus, reveals not only one of the earliest formulations of Christ's nature, but also conveys an apologetic motif in relating all of this theology to the vindication provided by Jesus' resurrection (cf. Acts 2:22f.).

Another early creed which links the resurrection with the person and claims of Jesus is Rom. 10:9-10.[37] In this passage, belief in this historical event is connected with confessing that Jesus is Lord. As a result one's salvation is secure.[38] Earlier it was pointed out that this may actually be a baptismal creed, whereby the candidate announced his belief in (and allegiance to) Jesus Christ.

Lastly, some creeds also confess Jesus' ascension to heaven and his resulting exaltation. Two examples of such early creeds were mentioned earlier with regard to the life of Jesus. In 1 Tim. 3:16, it is proclaimed that, after his incarnation, Jesus was "taken up in glory." In Phil. 2:6f. it is related that after Jesus humbled himself as a man, he was highly exalted and is to be worshipped by all persons (2:9-11).[39] This latter passage is taken from Isa. 45:23 where God the Father is receiving such praise and glory.

Before proceeding to the extended examination of 1 Cor. 15:3ff. it will be advantageous to briefly summarize the facts reported in various other creeds concerning the death and resurrection of Jesus. In addition to the events of his life, we are further informed that (6) Jesus attended a dinner (7) on the evening of his betrayal. (8) He gave thanks before the meal and (9) shared both bread and drink, (10) which, he declared, represented his imminent atoning sacrifice for sin (1 Cor. 11:23ff.). (11) Later, Jesus stood before Pilate and made a good confession, (12) which very possibly concerned his identity as the King of the Jews (1 Tim. 6:13). (13) Afterward, Jesus was killed for mankind's sins (1 Pet. 3:18; Rom. 4:25; 1 Tim. 2:6), (14) in spite of his righteous life (1 Pet. 3:18). (15) After his death he was resurrected (Luke 24:34; 2 Tim. 2:8). (16) It was asserted that this event validated Jesus' person and message (Rom. 1:3-4; 10:9-10). (17) After his resurrection, Jesus ascended to heaven and was glorified and exalted (1 Tim. 3:16; Phil. 2:6f.).

B. 1 Cor. 15:3ff.

While the subject of early Christian creeds is a fascinating area of research, some may wonder on what grounds the facts of the creeds themselves may be established. One approach to this question is to validate the New Testament documents as reliable sources and then argue to the creeds as trustworthy testimony. Although we have provided much of the grounds for such a response in Chapters II-III, in particular, and while this writer believes that such an answer is certainly the best approach (see Introduction), we are again reminded that the task we have set up for ourselves is to pursue *independent* evidence for such claims. Therefore, because of this particular goal, we will endeavor to provide special evidence for the death and resurrection of Jesus by referring to what is perhaps the most important single creed in the New Testament.

In 1 Cor. 15:3-4, Paul states:

> For I delivered to you as of first importance what I also received, that Christ died for our sins in accordance with the scriptures, that he was buried, that he was raised on the third day in accordance with the scriptures.[40]

As the passage continues, Paul records appearances of the resurrected Christ to Peter, to the "twelve" disciples, to over 500 persons at one time, to James, to all of the apostles and then to Paul himself (vv. 5-8). That this confession is an early Christian, pre-Pauline creed is recognized by virtually all critical scholars across a very wide theological spectrum.[41] There are several indications which reveal this conclusion. First, Paul's words "delivered" and "received" are technical terms for passing on tradition. As such, we have Paul's statement that this material was not his own, but received from another source.[42] Second, a number of words in this creed are non-Pauline, again indicating another origin of this material.[43] Jeremias, a leading authority on this issue, notes such non-Pauline phrases as (1) "for our sins" (v. 3); (2) "according to the scriptures" (vv. 3-4); (3) "he has been raised" (v. 4); (4) the "third day" (v. 4); (5) "he was seen" (vv. 5-8); and (6) "the twelve" (v. 5).[44] Third, it is likely that the creed is organized in a stylized, parallel form, thereby providing a further indication of the oral and confessional nature of this material.[45] Fourth, there are indications that there may be a Semitic original, such as the use of the Aramaic "Cephas" for Peter (v. 5), hence pointing to an earlier source before Paul's Greek translation.[46]

How early is this creed? Numerous critical theologians have endeavored to answer this important question, with very striking results. Ulrich Wilckens asserts that this creed "indubitably goes back to the oldest phase of all in the history of primitive Christianity."[47] Joachim Jeremias calls it "the earliest tradition of all."[48] Concerning a more exact time, it is very popular to date this creed in the mid-30s A.D. More specifically, numerous critical theologians date it from three to eight years after Jesus' crucifixion.[49]

How would Paul have received this creed? A number of scholars have arrived at the same scenario. Dating Jesus' crucifixion around 30 A.D., Paul's conversion would have occurred shortly after, about 33-35 A.D. Three years after his conversion (36-38 A.D.) he visited Jerusalem and specifically met with Peter and James (Gal. 1:18-19). It is therefore reasoned that the gospel of the death and resurrection of Jesus would in all likelihood be the normal center of discussion,[50] and that the presence of both Peter and James in the list of appearances (1 Cor. 15:5, 7) indicates the probability that Paul received this creed from these apostles when he visited them in Jerusalem.[51] Another possibility is that Paul received this material in Damascus immediately after his conversion, which would make it even three years earlier, but the presence of the Semitisms in the creed, as mentioned above, in addition to the two proper names, favor Jerusalem as the location where Paul first received it.

A Jerusalem location would date Paul's reception of the creed at about five to seven years after the crucifixion. But we can actually proceed back two stages earlier. Since the tradition would actually have been formulated before Paul first heard it, the creed itself would be dated even earlier. Additionally, the independent beliefs themselves, which later composed the formalized creed, would then date back to the actual historical events themselves. Therefore, we are dealing with material that proceeds *directly* from the events in question and this creed is thus crucial in our discussion of the death and resurrection of Jesus.

Not only are these facts reported *early*, but they are reported directly by the *eyewitnesses* themselves. Paul states that he specifically checked out his message with the apostles (Gal. 2:1-10) and he probably received this creed directly from these eyewitnesses themselves (Gal. 1:18-19), as already noted. As a direct result, not only had Paul personally seen the risen Christ (1 Cor. 15:8-9), but his testimony concerning the facts of the gospel agreed with that of the apostolic eyewitnesses (vv. 11, 14, 15).[52] Thus, Paul's factual account was the same as that of the other apostles, in spite of the fact that Paul distinguished himself from the others.[53]

As a result of this early and eyewitness testimony, the Christian teachings concerning the death, burial and resurrection of Jesus are open to historical testing. As German historian Hans von Campenhausen attests concerning 1 Cor. 15:3ff., "This account meets all the demands of historical reliability that could possibly be made of such a text."[54] A. M. Hunter states that "The passage therefore preserves uniquely early and verifiable testimony. It meets every reasonable demand of historical reliability."[55]

Now we begin to perceive the immense importance of this creed in terms of both facts and faith. Initially, it reveals some crucial facts concerning the gospel of the deity, death, burial and resurrection of Jesus. It also shows that Paul was very close to these facts.[56] As Dodd asserts concerning this creed:

> Thus Paul's preaching presents a special stream of Christian tradition which was derived from the mainstream at a point very near to its source. ...anyone who should maintain that the primitive Christian gospel was fundamentally different from that which we have found in Paul must bear the burden of proof.[57]

This factual witness to the death and resurrection of Jesus also became an apologetic for Christian belief.[58] The belief that the same Jesus who was dead and buried was raised again (1 Cor. 15:3-4) also strongly implies the empty tomb, especially in the context of Jewish thought.[59] On the other hand, this creed is also referred to by some as the most important single formulation of faith in the early church.[60]

The importance of the creed in 1 Cor. 15:3ff. can hardly be overestimated. No longer can it be charged that there is no demonstrable early, eyewitness testimony for the resurrection or for the other most important tenets of Christianity, for this creed provides just such evidential data concerning the facts of the gospel, which are the very center of the Christian faith. It links the events themselves with those who actually participated in time and space. As such this creed yields a strong factual basis for Christianity through the early and eyewitness reports of the death, burial and resurrection of Jesus, as will be shown in more detail in the next section of this chapter. For now we will only point out that naturalistic theories fail to account for this data. Additionally, the evidence demonstrates that these witnesses actually did see the risen Jesus, as they claimed. For instance, the fact that it was the original eyewitnesses who reported these events indicates that legends from a later period cannot explain this initial testimony.[61]

C. Known historical facts

Because of the testimony of these early Christian creeds, as well as other data, even contemporary critical scholars recognize a certain amount of historical facts surrounding the death, burial and resurrection of Jesus. In other words, even treating the New Testament as nothing more than a book of ancient literature, critics have deduced numerous historical facts concerning Jesus' life. These early creeds, and 1 Cor. 15:3ff., in particular, have played a significant part in this reconstruction.

There are a minimum amount of facts agreed upon by practically all critical scholars, whatever their school of thought. At least twelve separate facts are considered to be knowable history.

(1) Jesus died by crucifixion and (2) was buried. (3) Jesus' death caused the disciples to despair and lose hope, believing that his life was ended. (4) Although not as widely accepted, many scholars hold that the tomb in which Jesus was buried was discovered to be empty just a few days later.

Critical scholars further agree that (5) the disciples had experiences which they believed were literal appearances of the risen Jesus. Because of these experiences, (6) the disciples were transformed from doubters who were afraid to identify themselves with Jesus to bold proclaimers of his death and resurrection. (7) This message was the center of preaching in the early church and (8) was especially proclaimed in Jerusalem, where Jesus died and was buried shortly before.

As a result of this preaching, (9) the church was born and grew, (10) with Sunday as the primary day of worship. (11) James, who had been a skeptic, was converted to the faith when he also believed he saw the resurrected Jesus. (12) A few years later, Paul was also converted by an experience which he, likewise, believed to be an appearance of the risen Jesus.

These facts are crucial for our contemporary investigation of Jesus' resurrection. With the exception of the empty tomb, virtually all critical scholars who deal with this issue agree that these are a minimum of known historical facts surrounding this event. As such, any conclusion concerning the historicity of the resurrection should properly account for these facts. An additional vital (and major) function of these known historical facts will be explained below (see Section D).

These known historical facts have a twofold part in our case for the resurrection which is developed in this section. First, they answer the various theories which have been proposed in order to account for Jesus' resurrection on naturalistic grounds. These hypotheses, chiefly popularized by liberal scholars in the nineteenth century in particular, are rarely held today by critics, especially since they failed to account for the historical facts surrounding this event (such as those just mentioned above). Several reasons for this rejection could be enumerated.

Each naturalistic theory is beset by many major objections which invalidate it as a viable hypothesis. Combinations of these improbable theories likewise fail, again on factual grounds.[62] Three other historical reasons also illustrate this initial major point. David Hume's essay against miracles, as well as more recent updates, are invalid rejections of the possibility of miraculous events, thereby eliminating such reasoning as the traditional backdrop for these alternative theses.[63] Nineteenth century liberal scholars themselves destroyed each alternative theory individually,[64] while twentieth century critical scholars of various schools of thought have rejected these theories wholesale.[65] In conclusion, naturalistic alternative hypotheses have thereby been shown to be unable to account for the facts concerning Jesus' resurrection.

This leads to the second major argument for the resurrection based on the known historical facts. Not only have the naturalistic theories been disproven, but these same facts also establish numerous positive evidences which corroborate the historical and literal nature of this event. Nine such evidences will be listed here, all of which have been taken from our list of accepted historical facts listed above. Thus, the factual basis for these nine evidences is admitted by virtually all scholars. However, because of the limitations of this chapter, these nine will simply be stated with very little elaboration.

The key evidence for Jesus' resurrection is (1) the *disciples' experiences,* which they believed to be literal appearances of the risen Jesus, since these experiences cannot be explained by naturalistic theories (as just shown) and because they are attested as both early and eyewitness sources, as pointed out above. Other positive evidences include (2) the *transformation of the disciples into bold witnesses*, (3) the *empty tomb* and (4) the fact that the resurrection of Jesus was the very *center of the apostolic message*, all of which require adequate explanations. It was also found that the disciples proclaimed this message in Jerusalem itself, where it is related that in repeated confrontations with the authorities, (5) the *Jewish leaders could not disprove their message* (Acts 1-5). Additionally, (6) the very existence and growth of the *church*, (7) featuring *Sunday* as the primary day of worship demand historical causes, as well.

Two additional major facts arguing for the historicity of the resurrection are that two skeptics, (8) *James*, the brother of Jesus, and (9) *Paul*, became believers after having experiences which they also believed were appearances of the risen Jesus. Fuller concludes that even if the appearance to James had not been recorded by Paul (1 Cor. 15:7), such an occurrence would still have to be postulated anyway in order to account for both James' conversion and his subsequent promotion to a position of authority in the early church.[66] The same could be said even more emphatically concerning Paul.[67]

When combined with the failure of the naturalistic theories, this minimum of nine evidences provides a strong case for the historicity of Jesus' resurrection. This is especially so in that each of these evidences was based on a known historical fact.[68] In particular, when the early and eyewitness experiences of the disciples, James and Paul, are considered along with their corresponding transformations,[69] the historical resurrection becomes the best explanation for the facts, especially since the naturalistic theories failed.

D. "Core" historical facts

Earlier, twelve facts were enumerated as knowable history, accepted as such by almost all scholars. It is this writer's conviction that even by utilizing only four of these accepted facts, a sufficient case can be made for the historicity of the resurrection, which will strengthen the earlier apologetic.[70] The four facts to be used here are Jesus' death due to crucifixion, the subsequent experiences that the disciples were convinced were literal appearances of the risen Jesus, the corresponding transformation of the disciples and Paul's conversion experience, which he also believed was an appearance of the risen Jesus. These four "core" facts are even more widely accepted by virtually all critical scholars as knowable history.[71]

Each of these four facts is established by means of normal historical methodology (see Chapter I). The *death* of Jesus due to crucifixion is witnessed to not only by 1 Cor. 15:3, but is further corroborated by the nature of crucifixion (including Yohanan's skeleton), medical testimony concerning Jesus' heart wound, Strauss' famous critique of the swoon theory and the Shroud of Turin (see Chapter III,C for details). The fact of the disciple's *experiences*, which they believed to be appearances of the risen Jesus, is corroborated chiefly by the early and eyewitness testimony of 1 Cor. 15:3ff., as noted above. Additionally, since naturalistic theories have failed and the entire New Testament confirms this early eyewitness creed, the evidence for these experiences is generally considered by critical scholars to be as firmly established as almost any fact in the life of Jesus. In short, it is admitted by virtually all that the disciples had real experiences which caused them to believe that Jesus was raised from the dead.[72]

The *transformation* of the disciples as a result of these experiences is confirmed by the material immediately following this early creed (1 Cor. 15:9-11), which reports the ministry of the eyewitnesses. Again, the entire New Testament also verifies this conclusion, as does the testimony of the early church authors,[73] including the reports of the disciples dying for their faith as martyrs.[74] Lastly, *Paul's conversion* due to an experience that he also believed to be an appearance of the risen Jesus, is both reported by him personally in 1 Cor. 15:8-10 and validated by the writing of Paul's epistles, where he gives ample testimony of this fact. Therefore, the four core facts are established on strong, historical grounds. They are generally accepted not only by critical theologians but also by historians and philosophers who study this subject.[75]

Of these four core facts, the nature of the disciples' experiences is the most crucial. As historian Michael Grant asserts, historical investigation actually proves that the earliest eyewitnesses were convinced that they had seen the risen Jesus.[76] Carl Braaten adds that other skeptical historians also agree with this conclusion:

Even the more sceptical historians agree that for primitive Christianity ...the resurrection of Jesus from the dead was a real event in history, the very foundation of faith, and not a mythical idea arising out of the creative imagination of believers.[77]

One major advantage of these core facts is that, not only are they critically accepted as knowable history, but they directly concern the nature of the disciples' experiences. As such, these four historical facts are able, on a lesser scale, to both disprove the naturalistic theories and to provide major positive evidences which relate the probability of Jesus' literal resurrection.[78] A few examples will now point out these claims.

First, using only these four core historical facts, the naturalistic theories can be disproven. For instance, the swoon theory is ruled out by the facts concerning Jesus' death and by Paul's conversion. The disciples' experiences disprove the hallucination and other subjective theories both because such phenomena are not collective or contagious, being observed by one person alone, and because of the wide variety of time and place factors involved. The psychological preconditions for hallucinations were also lacking in these men. Paul's experience also rules out these theories because he certainly would not be in the proper psychological frame of mind. That it was the disciples and other early eyewitnesses who had these experiences likewise rules out legend or myth theories, since the original teaching concerning the resurrection is therefore based on the testimony of real eyewitnesses and not on later legends (as shown by the creed in 1 Cor. 15:3ff.). Paul's experience likewise cannot be explained by legends, since such could not account for his conversion from skepticism. Lastly, the stolen body and fraud theories are disproven by the disciples' experiences and by their transformation, both because this change shows that the disciples really believed that Jesus rose from the dead and because of the probability that such liars would not become martyrs. Similarly, Paul would not have been convinced by such fraud.[79]

Second, these four core facts also provide the major positive evidences for Jesus' literal resurrection appearances, such as the disciples' early and eyewitness experiences that have not been explained away naturalistically, their transformation into men who were willing to die for their faith and Paul's experience and corresponding transformation. Thus, these core historical facts provide positive evidences which further verify the disciples' claims concerning Jesus' literal resurrection, especially in that these arguments have not been accounted for naturalistically.[80]

Since these core historical facts (and the earlier accepted facts in general) have been *established by critical and historical procedures*, contemporary scholars cannot reject this evidence simply by referring to "discrepancies" in the New Testament texts or to its general "unreliability." Not only are such critical claims refuted by evidence discussed in other chapters, but it has been concluded that the resurrection can be historically demonstrated *even when the minimum amount of historical facts are utilized.* Neither can it be concluded merely that "something" occurred which is indescribable due to naturalistic premises, or to the character of history or because of the "cloudiness" or "legendary character" of the New Testament texts. Neither can it be said that Jesus rose spiritually, but not literally. Again, these and other such views are refuted in that the *facts admitted by virtually all scholars as knowable history are adequate* to historically demonstrate the literal resurrection of Jesus according to probability.

In short, instead of stating what they believe we *cannot* know concerning the gospel accounts, critical scholars would do well to concentrate on what even they admit *can* be known about the texts at this point. Although Jesus was not photographed in his resurrection body for the benefit of the disciples, the factual basis is enough to show that Jesus' resurrection is by far the best historical explanation. While critical doubts may be present with regard to other issues in the New Testament, the accepted facts are sufficient in themselves to show that Jesus rose from the dead in a new, spiritual body. As mentioned in Chapter I, historical inquiry can yield certainty. The resurrection has remained established in the face of criticism for almost 2000 years. The various types of evidence for this event are outstanding, surpassing that of the great majority of ancient events. Sidestepping or rejecting the evidence *a priori* is invalid, as we have seen. There is, indeed, historical proof for this event.[81] Jesus did rise from the dead in real history.

E. Synopsis of creeds and facts

In this chapter we have investigated probably the strongest single category of evidence for the death and resurrection of Jesus. The data supplied by oral creeds which were circulated before the actual composition of the New Testament and, often corresponding to these creeds, the facts which critical scholars admit as knowable history, provide a formidable basis for knowledge about Jesus.

From these sources we find reports of some incidents of Jesus' life but especially numerous details concerning his death and resurrection. Jesus was a real flesh and blood person (Phil. 2:6; 1 Tim. 3:16; 1 John 4:2) who was physically born of the lineage of David (Rom. 1:3-4; 2 Tim. 2:8). One creed most likely implies Jesus' baptism (Rom. 10:9). We are also told that Jesus preached his message among men, which resulted in people believing his testimony (1 Tim. 3:16).

On the night Jesus was betrayed, he first attended a dinner, where he prayed and gave thanks before the meal. Afterward, Jesus passed out both bread and drink, which he referred to as the sacrifice of his body and blood for sin (1 Cor. 11:23ff.). Later, Jesus appeared before Pilate, where he made a good confession, which very possibly concerned his identity as the Messiah (1 Tim. 6:13).

In spite of the fact that Jesus was a righteous man (1 Pet. 3:18), he was crucified, dead (1 Cor. 15:3; Phil. 2:8; 1 Pet. 3:18; Rom. 4:25) and buried (1 Cor. 15:4). These events caused the disciples doubt and despair. On the third day after the crucifixion, the tomb was empty (1 Cor. 15:4, implied). Jesus was raised from the dead (Lk. 24:34; 2 Tim. 2:8) and appeared to numerous eyewitnesses who reported these appearances at a very early date (1 Cor. 15:4f.). Two of these eyewitnesses were formerly skeptics before their conversions—namely James (1 Cor. 15:7) and Paul (1 Cor. 15:8, 9). After his resurrection, Jesus ascended to heaven and was exalted (1 Tim. 3:15; Phil. 2:6).

The disciples were transformed by these experiences (cf. 1 Tim. 3:16) and made the gospel the very center of their early preaching (1 Cor. 15:1-4). The resurrection was the chief validation of Jesus' person and message (Rom. 1:3-4; 10:9-10). This preaching initially centered in Jerusalem, where Jesus had been killed. Here the church was born and grew, with Sunday as the chief day of worship.

Most of these facts are reported in early Christian creeds and actually predate the writing of the New Testament. Others are virtually unanimously accepted by critical scholars, usually because of these creeds and other early historical data. It should be pointed out that these latter, critical facts were not accepted in this chapter simply because critics also accept them, but because they are established by the facts, such as by the creeds that we investigated in this chapter and by the work of careful historical methodology.[82] Thus, critical scholars should not object to this data, since it is both validated by their methods and accepted by their cohorts.

F. Conclusion

Once again, this chapter has presented perhaps our strongest category of evidence, especially for the death and resurrection of Jesus. Admittedly, the amount of material in this section concerning the life and ministry of Jesus was not overwhelming. However, when we enter the "passion week" of Jesus' life prior to his crucifixion, the situation changes drastically.

The strength of the testimony for Jesus' death and resurrection comes from several facets of the evidence. First, the material in this chapter was quite *early*. These early Christian creeds predate the writing of the New Testament and hence give us our earliest look at data dealing with the life of Jesus. In the case of 1 Cor. 15:3ff. (and perhaps a few other examples) this material dates within a few years of the actual events.

Second, these creeds present eyewitness testimony for the facts which they report. Again, 1 Cor. 15:3ff. is the key here in that it links us with the apostles, such as Peter and James, as well as with Paul. Another example is Luke 24:34, which may also date to the earliest church and Peter, as noted above.

Third, the accepted facts enumerated in this chapter, and the *core facts* in particular, are not only established on strictly historical grounds but are recognized by virtually all critical scholars as well. The advantages here are that these facts provide a strong basis for belief in the death and resurrection of Jesus and, at the same time, should not be rejected since they are recognized on historical grounds. The facts which almost all scholars accept provide a strong basis for belief in Jesus' literal resurrection from the dead, especially in the absence of viable naturalistic theories.

On this basis, then, we may conclude that early Christian creeds and accepted historical facts present an exceptionally strong case for the historicity of the death and resurrection of Jesus in particular. They are sufficient both to disprove the alternative theories, to present strong evidences for these events, such as the early and eyewitness testimony, and to do so on the grounds of known history. Critical doubts in other areas cannot disprove and change these basic facts.

[1]See Oscar Cullmann, *The Earliest Christian Confessions*, transl. by J. K. S. Reid (London: Lutterworth Press, 1949), pp. 35, 38. This book is one of the best known works on this subject.

[2]Ibid., pp. 57-58, 63-64.

[3]Ibid., p. 32.

[4]Ibid., pp. 22-23, 28, 55, 57-62. Cf. Rudolf Bultmann, *Theology of the New Testament*, transl. by Kendrick Grobel (New York: Charles Scribner's Sons, 1951, 1952), vol. 1, pp. 27, 125, 131, 175, 298; Vernon Neufeld, *The Earliest Christian Confessions* (Grand Rapids: William B. Eerdmans Publishing Company, 1964), pp. 9, 49, 57, 61; Reginald Fuller, *The Foundations of New Testament Christology* (New York: Charles Scribner's Sons, 1965), pp. 204-206, 221-225, 248; Wolfhart Pannenberg, *Jesus—God and Man*, transl. by Lewis L. Wilkens and Duane A. Priebe (Philadelphia: The Westminster Press, 1968), pp. 366-367.

[5]Bultmann, *Theology of the New Testament*, ibid., vol. 1, pp. 49, 81; Joachim Jeremias, *The Eucharistic Words of Jesus*, transl. by Norman Perrin (London: SCM Press, LTD, 1966), p. 102; Neufeld, p. 145, cf. p. 128.

[6]See Cullmann, pp. 55, 58; C. F. D. Moule, *The Birth of the New Testament*, revised edition (New York: Harper and Row, Publishers, 1982), p. 247; Neufeld, pp. 128-129, 133.

[7]Cullmann, p. 55; Bultmann, *Theology of the New Testament*, vol. 1, p. 27; II, p. 121; Pannenberg, pp. 118, 283, 367; Neufeld, pp. 7, 50; cf. Dodd, *The Apostolic Preaching and Its Developments* (Grand Rapids: Baker Book House, 1980), p. 14.

[8]For example, see Bultmann, vol. 1, pp. 27, 50. Other such sources will be pursued later in this chapter.

[9]Moule, p. 247.

[10]Jeremias, p. 102; Neufeld, pp. 7, 9, 128.

[11]Jeremias, p. 132; cf. Bultmann, *Theology of the New Testament*, vol. 1, p. 176; 2, pp. 153, 156; Fuller, *Christology*, pp. 214, 216, 227, 239.

[12]Moule, pp. 33-35.

[13]Cullmann, p. 41.

[14]Jeremias, p. 112; Bultmann, *Theology of the New Testament*, vol. 1, pp. 81, 125; Neufeld, pp. 43, 140.

[15]Bultmann, vol. 1, p. 312; Neufeld, pp. 62, 68, 144.

[16]Moule, p. 38; Jeremias, pp. 101, 104-105.

[17]Jeremias, p. 101.

[18]Ibid., pp. 101, 104-105.

[19]Cullmann, p. 64; Moule, pp. 38-39; Neufeld, p. 52.

[20]Bultmann, *Theology of the New Testament*, vol. 1, p. 83.

[21]Martin Hengel, *The Atonement*, transl. by John Bowden (Philadelphia: Fortress Press, 1981), p. 53.

[22]Moule, p. 38.

[23]Bultmann, *Theology of the New Testament*, vol. 2, p. 121; Neufeld, pp. 20, 31.

[24]See Cullmann, pp. 25, 27.

[25]Ibid.; Bultmann, *Theology of the New Testament*, vol. 1, p. 83.

[26]Neufeld, pp. 31, 63-64, 146.

[27]Ibid., p. 114; cf. pp. 132-133.

[28]Bultmann, *Theology of the New Testament*, vol. 1, p. 82.

[29]Cullmann, pp. 41, 45, 53, 57-62, including the creedal nature of these two references.

[30]Joachim Jeremias, "Easter: The Earliest Tradition and the Earliest Interpretation" in his *New Testament Theology*, transl. by John Bowden (New York: Charles Scribner's Sons, 1971), p. 306.

[31]C. H. Dodd, "The Appearances of the Risen Christ: An Essay in Form-Criticism of the Gospels" in his *More New Testament Studies* (Grand Rapids: William B. Eerdman's Publishing Company, 1968), p. 125; Bultmann, *Theology of the New Testament*, vol. 1, p. 45.

[32]Cf. Neufeld, pp. 7, 50; Pannenberg, pp. 118, 283, 367; Dodd, *Apostolic Preaching*, p. 14; Bultmann, *Theology of the New Testament*, vol. 1, p. 27; vol. 2, p. 121; Fuller, *Christology*, pp. 187, 189.

[33]Neufeld, p. 50.

[34]Cullmann, p. 55; Moule, p. 247.

[35]Cf. Moule, p. 247; Neufeld, pp. 51-52; Pannenberg, pp. 31, 133, 137, 147, 367; Bultmann, *Theology of the New Testament*, vol. 1, pp. 27, 50; Fuller, *Christology*, pp. 180, footnote 81, 187.

[36]Cullmann, pp. 55, 57-62.

[37]Jeremias, *Eucharistic Words*, p. 112; Neufeld, pp. 43, 140, 143; Bultmann, *Theology of the New Testament*, vol. 1, pp. 81, 125.

[38]See Dodd, *Apostolic Preaching*, p. 11.

[39]Cullmann, pp. 57-62.

[40]Revised Standard Version

[41]See Reginald Fuller, *The Formation of the Resurrection Narratives* (New York: The Macmillan Company, 1971), p. 10; Oscar Cullmann, *The Early Church: Studies in Early Christian History and Theology*, ed. by A. J. B. Higgins (Philadelphia: The Westminster Press, 1966), p. 64; Pannenberg, p. 90; Ulrich Wilckens, *Resurrection*, transl. by A. M. Stewart (Edinburgh: The Saint Andrew Press, 1977), p. 2; Hengel, pp. 36-38, 40; Bultmann, *Theology of the New Testament*, vol. 1, pp. 45, 80, 82, 293; Willi Marxsen, *The Resurrection of Jesus of Nazareth*, transl. by Margaret Kohl (Philadelphia: Fortress Press, 1970), pp. 80, 86; Hans Conzelmann, *1 Corinthians*, transl. by James W. Leitch (Philadelphia: Fortress Press, 1969), p. 251; Hans-Ruedi Weber, *The Cross*, transl. by Elke Jessett

(Grand Rapids: William B. Eerdmans Publishing Company, 1978), p. 58; Dodd, "Risen Christ," pp. 124-125; A. M. Hunter, *Bible and Gospel*, p. 108; Raymond E. Brown, *The Virginal Conception and Bodily Resurrection of Jesus* (New York: Paulist Press, 1973), pp. 81, 92; Norman Perrin, *The Resurrection According to Matthew, Mark and Luke* (Philadelphia: Fortress Press, 1977), p. 79; George E. Ladd, *I Believe in the Resurrection of Jesus* (Grand Rapids: William B. Eerdmans Publishing Company, 1975), p. 104; Neufeld, p. 47.

[42]Fuller, *Resurrection Narratives*, p. 10; Wilckens, p. 2; Bultmann, *Theology of the New Testament*, vol. 1, p. 293; Dodd, *Apostolic Preaching*, pp. 13-14; "Risen Christ," p. 125; Neufeld, p. 27; Brown, *Bodily Resurrection*, p. 81.

[43]Cullmann, *Early Church*, p. 64; Fuller, ibid., p. 10; Marxsen, p. 80; Weber, p. 59.

[44]Jeremias, pp. 101-102.

[45]See especially Fuller, *Resurrection Narratives*, pp. 11-12; Weber, p. 59; Jeremias, *Eucharistic Words*, pp. 102-103.

[46]Jeremias, in particular, provides a list of such Semitisms, ibid. (pp. 102-103). See also Pannenberg, p. 90; Fuller, ibid., p. 11; *Christology*, p. 160; Weber, p. 59.

[47]Wilckens, p. 2.

[48]Jeremias, "Easter," p. 306.

[49]For a sample of some of those who hold to these specific dates for this creed, see Cullmann, *The Early Church*, pp. 65-66; Pannenberg, p. 90; Dodd, *Apostolic Preaching*, p. 16; Hunter, *Jesus*, p. 100; Brown, *Bodily Resurrection*, p. 81; Fuller, *Christology*, pp. 142, 161; *Resurrection Narratives*, pp. 10, 14, 28, 48; Ladd, p. 105. O'Collins points out that, as far as he is aware, no scholars date this creed later than the 40s A.D. Even with such a date in the 40s, the general conclusions which we draw here, especially concerning the early and eyewitness testimony for the resurrection, still follow. See Gerald O'Collins, *What Are They Saying About the Resurrection?* (New York: Paulist Press, 1978), p. 112.

[50]It is interesting that when Paul returned to Jerusalem 14 years later, again meeting with Peter and James, the gospel *was* specifically mentioned as the center of the discussion (Gal. 2:1-10).

[51]See note 49 above, since each of these scholars also adopts this general framework.

[52]See Cullmann, *The Early Church*, pp. 65-66; cf. p. 73; Jeremias, *Eucharistic Words*, p. 106; Hengel, p. 38; Dodd, *Apostolic Preaching*, pp. 16-17.

[53]Cullmann, pp. 72-73.

[54]Hans von Campenhausen, "The Events of Easter and the Empty Tomb," in *Tradition and Life in the Church* (Philadelphia: Fortress Press, 1968), p. 44, as quoted by Ladd, p. 105.

[55]Hunter, *Jesus*, p. 100.

[56]Cullmann, *The Early Church*, p. 64; Jeremias, *Eucharistic Words*, p. 96; Pannenberg, p. 90; Dodd, *Apostolic Preaching*, p. 17.

[57]Dodd, p. 16.

[58]Bultmann, *Theology of the New Testament*, vol. 1, p. 295; Neufeld, pp. 66-67, 146.

[59]Cullmann, *Earliest Confessions*, p. 32, Wolfhart Pannenberg, "A Dialogue on Christ's Resurrection," in *Christianity Today*, 12/14, April 12, 1968, pp. 9-11.

[60]Weber, p. 58; Hengel, p. 37.

[61]Pannenberg, *Jesus*, p. 91.

[62]For details, see Gary R. Habermas, *The Resurrection of Jesus: A Rational Inquiry* (Ann Arbor: University Microfilms, 1976), pp. 114-171, in particular.

[63]Numerous excellent critiques of Hume and more recent updates have appeared, exposing the invalidity of such attempts. For examples, see C. S. Lewis, *Miracles* (New York: Macmillan Press, 1961); Richard Swinburne, *The Concept of Miracle* (London: Macmillan and St. Martin's Press, 1970); Werner Schaaffs, *Theology, Physics and Miracles*, transl. by Richard L. Renfield (Washington, D.C.: Canon Press, 1974); Gary R. Habermas, "Skepticism: Hume" in Norman L. Geisler, editor, *Biblical Errancy: An Analysis of its Philosophical Roots* (Grand Rapids: Zondervan Publishing House, 1981). See the discussion of Chapter I, C as well.

[64]For details, including a listing of primary sources from these nineteenth century rejections of each others' views, see Habermas, *The Resurrection of Jesus: A Rational Inquiry*, pp. 286-293. See Chapter II, C for a brief discussion of this point.

[65]For examples, see Karl Barth, *Church Dogmatics*, ed. by G. W. Bromiley and T. F. Torrance (Edinburgh: T. and T. Clark, 1956), vol. 4, part 1, p. 340; Raymond E. Brown, "The Resurrection and Biblical Criticism," *Commonweal*, November 24, 1967, especially p. 233; Pannenberg, *Jesus*, pp. 88-97; Wilckens, pp. 117-119; Günther Bornkamm, *Jesus of Nazareth*, transl. by Irene and Fraser McLuskey with James M. Robinson (New York: Harper and Row, Publishers, 1960), pp. 181-185.

[66]Fuller, *Resurrection Narratives*, p. 37. See also Wilckens, p. 113.

[67]Ibid., pp. 37, 46-47.

[68]As mentioned above, this is with the exception of the empty tomb, which is accepted by many scholars as historical. For an excellent defense of this fact, see Robert H. Stein, "Was the Tomb Really Empty?" in the *Journal of the Evangelical Theological Society* 20 (1977), pp. 23-29.

[69]This does not even include the experience of the more than 500 persons who also claimed to have seen the risen Jesus, concerning whom Paul asserted that most were still alive and could be questioned.

[70]The advantage of using only four of the facts is that, with such a small number, there is even a wider support for those facts among critical scholars. Additionally, these four reveal how strong the case for the resurrection is, in actuality.

[71]For a sampling of critical theologians who accept these four core facts, see Fuller, *Resurrection Narratives*, especially pp. 27-49; Bultmann, *Theology of the New Testament*, vol. 1, pp. 44-45; Paul Tillich, *Systematic Theology* (Chicago: The University of Chicago Press, 1951, 1957, 1963), vol. 2, pp. 153-158; Bornkamm, pp. 179-186; Wilckens, pp. 112-113; Pannenberg, *Jesus*, pp. 88-106; Jürgen Moltmann, *Theology of Hope*, transl. by James W. Leitch (New York: Harper and Row, Publishers, 1967), especially pp. 197-202; Hunter, *Jesus*, pp. 98-103; Perrin, pp. 78-84; Brown, *Bodily Resurrection*, especially pp. 81-92; Paul Van Buren, *The Secular Meaning of the Gospel* (New York: The Macmillan Company, 1963), pp. 126-134.

[72]Compare the testimony of historian Michael Grant (p. 176) with that of theologian Rudolf Bultmann, *Theology*, vol. 1, p. 45), who agree at this point with scholarship as a whole.

[73]For instance, see Clement's, *Corinthians* 42; *Barnabas* 5.

[74]See Eusebius, Book II: IX, XXIII; XXV.

[75]See note 71 above. See also Michael Grant, especially pp. 175-178; W. T. Jones, *The Medieval Mind* (New York: Harcourt, Brace, Jovanovich, Inc., 1969), pp. 34-35; Carl Braaten, *History and Hermeneutic* (Philadelphia: The Westminster Press, 1966), p. 78.

[76]Grant, p. 176.

[77]Braaten, p. 78.

[78]See Gary R. Habermas, *The Resurrection of Jesus: An Apologetic*, (Grand Rapids: Baker Book House, 1980), Chapter I for this argument in expanded form, including support for these facts.

[79]Expansions of these critiques and many additional refutations gathered from the larger list of accepted facts in Section C cannot be presented here. For a more complete treatment of these and other such alternative theories, see Habermas, *The Resurrection of Jesus: A Rational Inquiry*, pp. 114-171.

[80]The additional accepted facts in Section C also provide other significant arguments for this event, such as the other six evidences listed there.

Perhaps an illustration utilizing a court case will be helpful on this last point. We will postulate that more than a dozen eyewitnesses clearly observed some events which involved seeing a person perform a series of acts on various occasions. This testimony both came immediately after the occurrences themselves and the eyewitnesses were firm in their claims, as evidenced at numerous points. Further, the defendant and his assistants could not disprove the testimony even after literally years of research, in spite of their interest in doing so. No lying, collusion or other fraud, hallucinations or any other means of fakery or misconception could be established. Admittedly, quite a strong case would be made that this person in question was, in fact, seen by these persons at those places and times. But even more revealing, the prosecutor was able to build a limited but demonstrable case based only on the facts which the defendant, his assistants and their client admitted to be valid. Thus he was able to establish his argument based on their antagonistic testimony alone. Theoretically, would the jury be satisfied if the defendant pleaded that "Maybe the witnesses did not really see his client for some unknown reason in spite of the evidence" or, "It's not really important whether they saw him or not"? Clearly these would be inappropriate responses because the testimony reveals that the eyewitnesses did, in fact, literally see the person.

However, evidence for Jesus' resurrection is actually superior to this. To be sure, as with the court case, people must make a decision about this event, but unlike the court case, their decision does not determine the issue. The historical fact is established on the evidence alone and not by any decision. To object that court cases and evidence cannot be applied to miracle-claims such as the resurrection is to reject miracles unjustly or even *a priori*, as refuted in Chapters 1-2. And it is here that the evidence for the resurrection reveals that the earliest eyewitnesses did see the risen Jesus, as well as the literal nature of these appearances. Critical attempts fail at this point.

[81]It should be mentioned here that the New Testament asserts that the believer is given an assurance of this event (as well as other truths of God) by the witness of the Holy Spirit (Rom. 8:16; 1 John 5:9-13). Believers need not rely on investigations of critical hermeneutical methodology, as was done here. Such processes can confirm what is already certified, however, or answer the questions of skeptics.

[82]See Michael Grant's *Jesus: An Historian's View of the Gospels*, for an example of a critical historical work which uncovers other such early data (in addition to the creeds) concerning the life of Jesus. Again, Grant also recognizes the four core facts (pp. 175-178). See Sherwin-White's *Roman Society and Roman Law in the New Testament* for an instance of another ancient historian who also uses critical methodology and applies it to the trial of Jesus and the journeys of Paul, in particular. Interestingly, Sherwin-White finds that the appropriate New Testament texts are very trustworthy at these points (see pp. 186-193), as we indicated especially in Chapter II above.

6

Ancient Christian Sources
(Non-New Testament)

In addition to the New Testament, early Christian writers produced volumes of important works which give valuable insight into early Christian beliefs, doctrines, and customs, as well as various types of exhortation. Many of these writings also contain brief statements concerning the historicity of Jesus. Our purpose in this chapter is not to investigate all of these statements concerning Jesus, but to study only those passages which exhibit an explicitly historical interest. Because of this emphasis on the historically oriented claims, our treatment of these ancient Christian sources will be comparatively brief despite the large number of works which fit into this category.[1] We begin with the earlier writers, usually referred to as the "apostolic fathers" (about 90-125 A.D.),[2] and then present some historical statements in the writings of Justin Martyr, which immediately followed this earlier period.

A. 90-125 A.D.

Clement of Rome. One of the most important apostolic documents, Clement of Rome's letter to the Corinthian church is generally considered to be the earliest extra-New Testament Christian writing. Clement was the leading elder in the church at Rome and wrote *Corinthians* about 95 A.D. to help end a dispute between the laity and elders at Corinth.

Although *Corinthians* is largely doctrinal and moral in nature, it contains at least one important historical reference to Jesus and earliest Christianity:

The Apostles received the Gospel for us from the Lord Jesus Christ; Jesus Christ was sent forth from God. So then Christ is from God, and the Apostles are from Christ. Both therefore came of the will of God in the appointed order. Having therefore received a charge, and having been fully assured through the resurrection of our Lord Jesus Christ and confirmed in the word of God with full assurance of the Holy Ghost, they went forth with the glad tidings that the kingdom of God should come. So preaching everywhere in country and town, they appointed their firstfruits, when they had proved them by the Spirit, to be bishops and deacons unto them that should believe.[3]

In this passage, Clement of Rome claims several facts. (1) The gospel or good news of the Kingdom of God was the major Christian message. (2) This gospel had been given to the apostles by Jesus himself even as it came from God. (3) Jesus' resurrection provided the assurance of the truthfulness of these teachings. (4) With the additional certainty of Scripture, the apostles spread the gospel. (5) Wherever the gospel was preached and local congregations were started, leaders were chosen to minister to the believers.

This certification of a chain of authority from God to Jesus to the apostles to the early Christian elders is interesting not only in that it was the basis for early doctrinal proclamation and church organization. Additionally, Clement of Rome anchors this authority in the belief that Jesus was raised from the dead and in the Scripture. A miraculous event in history was thus taken as the basic sign of authority behind the preaching of the earliest Christian message.

Ignatius. As bishop of Antioch and a leader in the early church, Ignatius was condemned to death in Rome. On the way to his execution he addressed seven letters to six chuches and one individual (Polycarp). These letters are early witnesses to Christian doctrine and to early church hierarchy, being written about 110-115 A.D. They also contain several historical references to Jesus. In his epistle to the *Trallians*, Ignatius states:

> Jesus Christ who was of the race of David, who was the Son of Mary, who was truly born and ate and drank, was truly persecuted under Pontius Pilate, was truly crucified and died in the sight of those in heaven and on earth and those under the earth; who moreover was truly raised from the dead, His Father having raised Him, who in the like fashion will so raise us also who believe on Him.[4]

In this portion, Ignatius affirms several facts concerning Jesus. (1) He was of the lineage of David and (2) born of Mary. (3) As such, he really lived, ate and drank on the earth. (4) Jesus was crucified and died at the

142

hands of Pontius Pilate. (5) Afterward God raised him from the dead, (6) as an example of the believer's resurrection. Again we perceive how the resurrection was the chief sign for believers, in this case that they would be raised from the dead like Jesus.

In his epistle to the *Smyrneans*, Ignatius refers twice to the historical Jesus. In the first instance, he asserts concerning Jesus:

> He is truly of the race of David according to the flesh, but Son of God by the Divine will and power, truly born of a virgin and baptised by John that *all righteousness might be fulfilled* by Him, truly nailed up in the flesh for our sakes under Pontius Pilate and Herod the tetrarch (of which fruit are we—that is, of His most blessed passion); that *He might set up an ensign* unto all ages through His resurrection.[5] (Emphasis added by the editor.)

Ignatius again affirms (7) that Jesus was physically of the lineage of David, adding (8) that he was also the Son of God as shown by the virgin birth. (9) Jesus was baptized by John, (10) later being nailed (crucified) under Pontius Pilate and Herod the tetrarch. (11) Afterward, Jesus was raised from the dead.

In a second reference in *Smyrneans*, Ignatius concentrates on Jesus' resurrection:

> For I know and believe that He was in the flesh even after the resurrection; and when He came to Peter and his company, He said to them, *Lay hold and handle me, and see that I am not a demon without body.* And straightway they touched him, and they believed, being joined unto His flesh and His blood. Wherefore also they despised death, nay they were found superior to death. And after His resurrection He [both] ate with them and drank with them.[6] (Emphasis added by the editor.)

Speaking of the resurrection, Ignatius affirms that Jesus (12) was raised in the flesh. (13) Afterward he appeared to Peter and the disciples and told them to touch his physical body, which they did. (14) Jesus then ate and drank with them after his resurrection. (15) In a statement reminiscent of Lucian, Ignatius also relates that upon believing, the disciples despised death.

A last reference which Ignatius makes concerning the historical Jesus is found in his epistle to the *Magnesians*:

> Be ye fully persuaded concerning the birth and the passion and the resurrection, which took place in the time of the governorship of Pontius Pi-

late; for these things were truly and certainly done by Jesus Christ our hope.[7]

Here Ignatius assures his readers that they can be certainly persuaded of the facticity of Jesus' (16) birth, (17) death and (18) resurrection, all of which occurred while Pontius Pilate was governor. As in the other references, Ignatius attempts to place such events firmly in the realm of history. His purpose, at least partially, is to provide an answer to the threat of gnosticism, which often denied physical interpretations of some of these events.

Quadratus. One of the early apologists to begin answering claims raised against Christianity, Quadratus addressed an apology to Emperor Hadrian about 125 A.D. Unfortunately, this work is presently known only from one statement preserved by Eusebius in the fourth century.

Eusebius relates that Quadratus wrote his apology in order to answer malicious claims meant to harass Christians. It is stated that this defense was both sound in doctrine and revealed Quadratus' knowledge of the situation. Then Eusebius quotes a sentence from Quadratus' apology:

> The deeds of our Saviour were always before you, for they were true miracles; those that were healed, those that were raised from the dead, who were seen, not only when healed and when raised, but were always present. They remained living a long time, not only whilst our Lord was on earth, but likewise when he had left the earth. So that some of them have also lived to our own times.[8]

This brief quotation from Quadratus' apology relates several important items concerning Jesus' miracles. (1) The facticity of Jesus' miracles could be checked by interested persons, since they were done publicly. With regard to the actual types of miracles, (2) some were healed and (3) some were raised from the dead. (4) There were eyewitnesses of these miracles at the time they occurred. (5) Many of those healed or raised were still alive when Jesus "left the earth" and some were reportedly still alive in Quadratus' own time.

B. 126-155 A.D.

Barnabas. The epistle of Barnabas (sometimes referred to as Pseudo-Barnabas) has explicit anti-legalistic overtones and expresses opposition to Judaism. Its purpose is to show that Jesus Christ is the fulfillment of the Old Testament law, but in doing so it often resorts to allegorical interpretations. Dates for this writing have varied widely, often from the late first century to the mid-second century. A commonly accepted date is 130-138 A.D.

In one major passage, *Barnabas* relates several facts concerning the life of Jesus:

> He must needs be manifested in the flesh....He preached teaching Israel and performing so many wonders and miracles, and He loved them exceedingly....He chose His own apostles who were to proclaim His Gospel....But He Himself desired so to suffer; for it was necessary for Him to suffer on a tree.[9]

From this portion we note (1) that Jesus became a man. He (2) preached and taught Israel, (3) performed miracles and (4) expressed love for the people. (5) Jesus chose his apostles (6) to proclaim the message of the gospel. (7) It was necessary for Jesus to suffer on a tree (crucifixion).

Justin Martyr. With the work of Justin Martyr, early Christian scholarship entered a new dimension. There is a marked difference between the characteristically devotional, doctrinal and practical exhortations of the apostolic writings and the apologetic works of Justin Martyr. These works reflect his personal philosophical pilgrimage and his own polemic interests, which led to his reputation as the major Christian apologist of the second century. Included in his works are a number of historical references to Jesus.

In his *First Apology*, written soon after 150 A.D. and addressed chiefly to Emperor Antoninus Pius, Justin Martyr refers to various aspects of the life of Jesus. Referring to Jesus' birth, it is noted that he was born of a virgin, while his physical line of descent came through the tribe of Judah and the family of Jesse.[10] Later, after mentioning the location of Jesus' birth in the town of Bethlehem, Justin explains:

> Now there is a village in the land of the Jews, thirty-five stadia from Jerusalem, in which Jesus Christ was born, as you can ascertain also from the registers of the taxing made under Cyrenius, your first procurator in Judea.[11]

These two references state several items surrounding Jesus' birth. (1) He was born of a virgin, (2) while he was a physical descendant of Jesse, of the tribe of Judah. (3) The village of Bethlehem was his birthplace, (4) which was located thirty-five stadia (approximately five miles) from Jerusalem. (5) The location and fact of Jesus' birth could be verified by consulting the records of Cyrenius, the first procurator of Judea.

Justin Martyr also refers to Jesus' public ministry and to the official documentation of his message. Earlier Justin's reference to the *Acts of Pontius Pilate* was discussed,[12] where it is asserted that Jesus' miracles such as his healing of diseases and raising the dead could be evidenced from Pilate's report.[13] Furthermore, in answer to the question as to whether Jesus did his miracles by magic, Justin answered in the negative, pointing to Jesus' fulfillment of prophecy as a vindication of his claims.[14] From these texts we note (6) that Jesus did miracles which were believed to be referenced in Pilate's report. (7) Fulfilled messianic prophecy was also taken as a further validation of his claims.

Justin also referred frequently to Jesus' death by crucifixion. On one occasion he spoke of Jesus as "Him who was crucified in Judea."[15] In a second reference to the so-called *Acts of Pontius Pilate*, he declares that Jesus was nailed to the cross through his hands and feet, and that some of those present cast lots for his clothing.[16] In a more extended reference to Jesus' death and resurrection, Justin Martyr declares:

> Accordingly, after He was crucified, even all His acquaintances forsook Him, having denied Him; and afterwards, when He had risen from the dead and appeared to them, and had taught them to read the prophecies in which all these things were foretold as coming to pass, and when they had seen him ascending into heaven, and had believed, and had received power sent thence by Him upon them, and went to every race of men, they taught these things, and were called apostles.[17]

In these three references Justin reports (8) that Jesus was nailed to the cross through his hands and feet and (9) was crucified (10) while his garments were taken from him. (11) His friends denied and forsook him. (12) Later, Jesus rose from the dead and appeared to his followers, (13) teaching them concerning the prophecies which he fulfilled. (14) After Jesus ascended to heaven, (15) those who believed in him went out preaching to all men and (16) were called apostles.

In another work, *Dialogue with Trypho*, Justin Martyr writes specifically for Jews, in order to convince them that Jesus is the Messiah. Here we also find several historical references to Jesus. For instance, Justin asserts:

For at the time of His birth, Magi who came from Arabia worshipped Him, coming first to Herod, who then was sovereign in your land.[18]

Here it is pointed out (17) that Arabian Magi visited Jesus at his birth and worshipped him, after (18) first stopping to see Herod, the ruler of the Jews.

Later, speaking of Jesus' crucifixion Justin writes:

For when they crucified Him, driving in the nails, they pierced His hands and feet; and those who crucified Him parted His garments among themselves, each casting lots for what he chose to have, and receiving according to the decision of the lot.[19]

Here Justin explicitly records several more events. He asserts (19) that Jesus was crucified, being nailed through both his hands and feet. (20) Again we find a reference to gambling for Jesus' clothes by those who crucified him, with each person keeping the items which he had won.

Following Jesus' death by crucifixion, the gospel of Matthew reports that the Jews spread the story that the disciples came and stole his dead body (Matt. 28:11-15). Justin explains that this story was still being proclaimed everywhere by the Jews:

Christ said amongst you that He would give the sign of Jonah, exhorting you to repent of your wicked deeds at least after He rose again from the dead...yet you not only have not repented, after you learned that he rose from the dead, but, as I said before, you have sent chosen and ordained men throughout all the world to proclaim that a godless and lawless heresy had sprung from one Jesus, a Galilean deceiver, whom we crucified, but his disciples stole him by night from the tomb, where he was laid when unfastened from the cross, and now deceive men by asserting that he has risen from the dead and ascended to heaven.[20]

This interesting portion reports (21) that Jesus predicted that he would rise ahead of time,[21] and (22) exhorted the Jews to repent. (23) Even after Jesus rose from the dead the Jews did not repent but (24) spread the story that the disciples stole Jesus' body after he was crucified, and that the disciples then lied about the resurrection. (25) The disciples also taught that Jesus afterward ascended to heaven, which at least witnesses to the early Christian belief in this occurrence.

Lastly, Justin Martyr also witnesses to the facticity of the resurrection in another portion of *Dialogue with Trypho*:

For indeed the Lord remained upon the tree almost until evening, and they buried Him at eventide; then on the third day He rose again.[22]

Here Justin records (26) that Jesus hung on the "tree" until evening,[23] (27) that he was buried at that time and (28) that he rose from the dead the third day afterward.

Justin Martyr records many other events from the life of Jesus, but often he reports that his data was gleaned from the Scripture.[24] These references here will suffice to provide numerous examples of Justin's interest in Jesus' actual life on earth.

C. Synopsis of Christian sources

In this chapter we have investigated five early Christian sources for the historicity of Jesus, all of which were extra-New Testament. Our intent was not to examine all the passages which spoke of Jesus, but only those which claimed to report historical data. Additionally, we limited our discussion to the life of Jesus, thereby overlooking material concerning early Christian origins. A synopsis of this material provides the listing of numerous details.

The Life of Jesus. These ancient Christian sources taught that Jesus really did live on earth in human history (Ignatius) after being born as a man (Barnabas). He was from the tribe of Judah (Justin), from the family of Jesse (Justin) and of the lineage of David (Ignatius). Jesus was born of Mary (Ignatius), a virgin (Ignatius, Justin), in the city of Bethlehem (Justin). It is even reported that Bethlehem was located about five miles from Jerusalem and that this birth could be verified by the records of Cyrenius, the first procurator of Judea (Justin). Later, he was visited by Arabian Magi, who had first visited Herod (Justin).

Concerning his public ministry, these sources record Jesus' baptism by John (Ignatius) and his choosing of apostles (Barnabas, Justin). There are also reports of miracles performed by Jesus (Quadratus, Barnabas, Justin). Here it is carefully pointed out that these miracles consisted of people being both healed and raised from the dead, concerning which it is asserted that some of the eyewitnesses to these events were still alive (Quadratus). It is also claimed that Pilate filed a report with the officials at Rome which corroborated these details (Justin). Additionally, we are told that Jesus fulfilled Old Testament prophecy, thereby validating his claims (Justin).

The Teachings of Jesus. These sources also record some of Jesus' important teachings. It is related that he preached and taught Israel, a people whom he loved (Barnabas). He exhorted the Jews to repent, yet they did not do so even after he rose from the dead, an event which Jesus had predicted ahead of time (Justin).

Jesus' major teaching was the nature of the gospel, which he received from God and later imparted to his apostles (Clement, Barnabas). It is asserted that the apostles were fully assured of the truthfulness of the message and that they, in turn, preached the Kingdom of God in various towns and countries. Where this message went, it was accompanied by the organizing of churches, complete with the choosing of leaders such as bishops and deacons (Clement).

The Death of Jesus. These early Christian writers were careful to point to the facticity of Jesus' death by crucifixion (Ignatius, Barnabas, Justin). They sought to link it firmly to history, such as with the assertion that this event occurred during the governorship of Pontius Pilate and the reign of Herod (Ignatius). Details of the crucifixion are also provided, such as Jesus being nailed to the cross (Ignatius, Justin) while his clothing was divided among his assassins (Justin). Jesus hung on the cross until evening, after which he was taken down and buried (Justin). During this period of time, his friends forsook and denied him (Justin).

The Resurrection of Jesus. These Christians were equally adamant in their belief that Jesus' resurrection is also a fact of history (Clement, Ignatius, Justin). This event occurred on the third day after Jesus' crucifixion in spite of the Jewish claim that the disciples stole the body (Justin).

Evidencing the fact that he had been raised from the dead, Jesus appeared to Peter and the other disciples (Ignatius, Justin). During these encounters, Jesus encouraged and even allowed the disciples to touch his risen flesh, which they did (Ignatius). Jesus also ate and drank with his followers (Ignatius) and taught them concerning how he had fulfilled Old Testament prophecy (Justin). Later, Jesus ascended to heaven (Justin, cf. Quadratus).

These early Christian authors asserted that Jesus' resurrection provided the assurance that the gospel which he preached was ordained by God (Clement). This event was an example of the believer's resurrection and was the reason why the disciples despised death (Ignatius).

D. Conclusion

What value do these early extra-New Testament sources have in reconstructing a historical life of Jesus? Do such Christian authors provide any exceptional evidence for the death and resurrection? Actually, there are both positive and negative considerations in such questions.

Positively, the Christian sources presented in this chapter are early. Clement wrote at the end of the first century, or at approximately the same time as some of the later New Testament writings. Ignatius' seven books date from about fifteen to twenty years later. These men were also close to apostolic sources, as is evident from their own works,[25] and from other early testimony.[26]

Another factor is that some of these early authors were scholars or leaders in their own right. Clement and Ignatius were well-known bishops in the early church,[27] while Justin was a rather distinguished philosopher.[28] Additionally, these writers were frequently careful to cite evidence for their assertions. Clement and Ignatius referred to the resurrection as the basis for Christian truth. Quadratus backed his testimony with eyewitness testimony concerning Jesus' miracles. Justin referred to miracles and fulfilled prophecy as evidence.

However, in spite of these early sources, scholarly testimonies and citings of evidence, there are also weaknesses in our usage of these sources. Initially, it is obvious that these writings rely on the New Testament for much of their data, as is specifically reported by Justin.[29] That they do so is certainly not a weakness in itself, for it was pointed out in Chapters II and III that the New Testament is a good historical source. However, the point is that if they rely on the New Testament, then they are not totally *extra*-New Testament, and the object of this work is to ascertain what evidence of this latter kind is available. It should also be remembered that the purpose of these writers was not a critical investigation of history per se, but the reporting of Christian origins. While such is certainly a valid approach, and can yield historical facts, additional evidence could certainly strengthen the case.

Such additional, corroborative data is partially available from the secular sources in Chapter IV. Many of the reports gleaned from those secular sources confirm the citings pointed out here, especially with regard to the teachings and crucifixion of Jesus. There are also parallels concerning his life and the reports of his resurrection. Our purpose in Part Two is to ascertain if there are additional ancient sources of data which continue to corroborate our development of an extra-biblical picture of Jesus' life.

[1]Therefore, some well-known works such as the *Shepherd of Hermas* will not be included in this discussion at all, since it contains little which might be counted as historical information concerning Jesus.

[2]Quotations from the apostolic fathers are taken from J. B. Lightfoot, editor and translator of *The Apostolic Fathers* (Grand Rapids: Baker Book House, 1891, 1956).

[3]Clement of Rome, *Corinthians*, 42.

[4]Ignatius, *Trallians*, 9.

[5]Ignatius, *Smyrneans*, 1.

[6]Ibid., 3.

[7]Ignatius, *Magnesians*, 11.

[8]Eusebius, IV: III.

[9]*Barnabas*, 5.

[10]Justin Martyr, *First Apology*, XXXII.

[11]Ibid., XXXIV. Quotations from the works of Justin Martyr are taken from the *Ante-Nicene Fathers*, ed. by Alexander Roberts and James Donaldson (Grand Rapids: William B. Eerdmans Publishing Company, 1973), vol. 3.

[12]See Chapter IV, F.

[13]Justin Martyr, *First Apology*, XLVIII.

[14]Ibid., XXX. For some specific Messianic prophecies, see XXXII-XXXV.

[15]Ibid., XXXII.

[16]Ibid., XXXV.

[17]Ibid., L.

[18]Justin Martyr, *Dialogue with Trypho*, LXXVII.

[19]Ibid., XCVII.

[20]Ibid., CVIII; cf. XVII.

[21]This is "the sign of the prophet Jonas" (see Matt. 12:38-40).

[22]*Dialogue with Trypho*, XCVII.

[23]Justin refers to it as a "cross" in CVIII, for instance.

[24]Cf. ibid., CV and CVI, for examples.

[25]See Ignatius, *Romans*, 4; cf. Clement, *Corinthians*, 47.

[26]For example, see Eusebius, III: XV-XVI.

[27]Ibid., III: XV-XXII.

[28]Ibid., IV: XVI.

[29]Cf. *Dialogue with Trypho*, CV and CVI.

7

Archaeological Sources

As pointed out in Chapter I, historical methodology includes the use of non-written as well as written sources. Archaeology is able to give much information about the past, in that it can both confirm and shed new light on known data and can establish evidence for facts on its own.

In this chapter we will attempt to point out some archaeological evidence which either corroborates or helps establish historical facts in the life of Jesus. To be sure, the amount of material here is not as abundant as is the support for portions of the Old Testament. Nonetheless, the examples which we use will generally be quite evidential, and thus we will continue to build a case for what can be known of Jesus from extra-biblical sources.

A. Luke's census

In Luke 2:1-5 we read that Caesar Augustus decreed that the Roman Empire should be taxed and that everyone had to return to his own city to pay taxes. So Joseph and Mary returned to Bethlehem and there Jesus was born.

Several questions have been raised in the context of this taxation. Is there any evidence that such a massive census ever took place? Even if such a taxation actually did occur, would every person have to return to his home? Was Quirinius really the governor of Syria at this time (as in v. 2)?[1] Archaeology has had a bearing on the answers to these questions.

It has been established that the taking of a census was quite common at about the time of Christ. An ancient Latin inscription called the *Titulus Venetus* indicates that a census took place in Syria and Judea about 5-6 A.D. and that this was typical of those held throughout the Roman Empire from the time of Augustus (23 B.C.-14 A.D.) until at least the third century A.D. Indications are that this census took place every fourteen years. Other such evidence indicates that these procedures were widespread.[2] Concerning persons returning to their home city for the taxation-census, an Egyptian papyrus dating from 104 A.D. reports just such a practice. This rule was enforced, as well.[3]

The question concerning Quirinius also involves the date of the census described in Luke 2. It is known that Quirinius was made governor of Syria by Augustus in 6 A.D. Archaeologist Sir William Ramsay discovered several inscriptions which indicated that Quirinius was governor of Syria on two occasions, the first time several years previous to this date.[4] Within the cycle of taxation-censuses mentioned above, an earlier taxation would be dated from 10-5 B.C.[5] Another possibility is Bruce's point that the Greek in Luke 2:2 is equally translatable as "This enrollment (census) was before that made when Quirinius was governor of Syria."[6] This would mean that Luke was dating the taxation-census before Quirinius took over the governorship of Syria. Either possibility answers the question raised above.

Therefore, while some questions have been raised concerning the events recorded in Luke 2:1-5, archaeology has provided some unexpected and supportive answers. Additionally, while supplying the background behind these events, archaeology also assists us in establishing several facts. (1) A taxation-census was a fairly common procedure in the Roman Empire and it did occur in Judea, in particular. (2) Persons were required to return to their home city in order to fulfill the requirements of the process. (3) These procedures were apparently employed during the reign of Augustus (37 B.C.-14 A.D.), placing it well within the general time frame of Jesus' birth. (4) The date of the specific taxation recounted by Luke could very possibly have been 6-5 B.C., which would also be of service in attempting to find a more exact date for Jesus' birth.

B. Yohanan—crucifixion victim

Most of this chapter pertains to archaeological evidence which bears on the issues of Jesus' death and resurrection. The first example of this concerns an important discovery made in June, 1968, which provides much information about the nature of crucifixion as it was exercised in first century A.D. Palestine. While a portion of Jerusalem was being prepared for the erection of new apartment buildings, an ancient Jewish burial site was uncovered. Located about one mile north of the Old Damascus Gate, this site yielded the remains of some thirty-five Jews, which were buried in fifteen stone ossuaries, used for the reburial of human skeletons some time after the original interment.

Upon investigation, archaeologist Vasilius Tzaferis found that these Jews had probably died about 70 A.D. in the Jewish uprising against Rome. Several of the skeletons gave evidence of having suffered violent deaths, such as being burned, starved or beaten to death. One person had been killed by an arrow.[7]

In terms of our study, the most important discovery at this site was the skeleton of a man named Yohanan Ben Ha'galgol, whose name was written in Aramaic on the stone ossuary. Yohanan was about five feet seven inches in height, was about twenty-four to twenty-eight years old, had a cleft palate and was a victim of crucifixion. Still piercing his feet was a large nail about seven inches long that had been driven sideways through his heel bones, which indicates the direction in which the feet and legs were twisted in order for them to be attached to the cross. The nail pierced an acacia wood wedge first, then went through the heels and into the upright beam of the cross, which was anchored in the ground. Small pieces of wood still attached to the spike indicated that the beam itself was olive wood. The end of the nail was bent backwards toward the head due either to a knot in the wood or to purposeful bending.

Further research by Hebrew University pathologist Dr. Nica Haas revealed even more data regarding Yohanan's skeleton. An examination disclosed the fact that nails had also been driven between the radius and ulna bones in the lower arm. The radius bone was both scratched and actually worn smooth. This latter result was apparently due to repeated friction caused by the crucifixion victim pulling himself upward in order to breathe, followed by sinking back down again. As the weight of the body was repeatedly moved in order to free the pectoral and intercostal muscles, which inhibit breathing in the "down" position, the radius was worn.

Additionally, Haas discovered that Yohanan's lower leg bones were broken. The left tibia and fibula bones and the right tibia bone were apparently crushed by a common blow, with the legs being sawed off at a later time. This is quite consistent with the dreaded Roman *crucifragium* spoken of in John 19:31-32 as being normal procedure for crucifixion victims. Death was hastened because the victim was not able to push himself up on the cross in order to breathe, which brought death in a comparatively short period of time.[8]

In this case the crucifixion process recorded in the Gospels has been largely corroborated by this new discovery. Once again we perceive how archaeology provides us with facts pertaining to the life of Jesus. (1) Victims were often nailed to crosses through the feet or heels and through the wrist-lower arm area. (2) The positioning of the body required the victim to move upward and downward in order to alternatively breathe and rest. (3) The executioners usually smashed the leg bones in order to render a hasty death in cases where the person did not die quickly enough. Likewise, Tacitus records some similar details.[9]

C. The Nazareth Decree

In 1878 a marble slab measuring approximately fifteen by twenty-four inches was discovered at Nazareth, describing itself as an "ordinance of Caesar." The message was a strict prohibition against the disturbing of graves. Scholars generally agree that it was issued by Claudius between 41-54 A.D. The inscription was written in Greek, translated as follows:

> Ordinance of Caesar. It is my pleasure that graves and tombs remain perpetually undisturbed for those who have made them for the cult of their ancestors or children or members of their house. If, however, anyone charges that another has either demolished them, or has in any other way extracted the buried, or has maliciously transferred them to other places in order to wrong them, or has displaced the sealing on other stones, against such a one I order that a trial be instituted, as in respect of the gods, so in regard to the cult of mortals. For it shall be much more obligatory to honor the buried. Let it be absolutely forbidden for anyone to disturb them. In case of violation I desire that the offender be sentenced to capital punishment on charge of violation of sepulchre.[10]

As noted by Maier, all previous Roman indictments of this nature prescribe only a fine for the offender, but this order demands capital punishment. Why should such a strong penalty be levied in Palestine?[11]

Although the exact reasoning is not known for sure, scholars have frequently suggested that such an order straight from the emperor can best be explained by the likelihood that Claudius investigated some of the beliefs of Christians after the riots that erupted around the Roman Empire during his reign, events associated with the spread of Christianity (see Acts 17:1-9, for example). Such an investigation would be especially likely in the case of Claudius because of these riots in Rome in 49 A.D., which caused the emperor to expel the Jews from the city. Suetonius remarks that the troubles were instigated by Christ.[12]

Upon examination, Claudius could well have discovered the Christian teaching that Jesus had risen from the dead and may also have heard the Jewish report that the disciples stole the body. This possiblity is made more significant due to the Nazareth Decree's mention of those who would disturb tombs that had been sealed. This is certainly reminiscient of Matt. 28:66, where we are told that the Jews were careful to seal the tomb of Jesus after permission was secured from Pilate. The Nazareth Decree could be a reaction both to the Christian teaching that Jesus was raised and the Jewish contention that the body was stolen.[13]

From this decree we may glean certain historical facts, irrespective of the exact occasion for the indictment. (1) Apparently there were reports in Palestine which caused the emperor (probably Claudius) to issue this stern warning against disturbing or robbing graves. (2) Jewish burial often included sealing the sepulchre as well as the use of stones. (3) The offense of grave robbing had now become a capital offense and was punishable by death.

D. Shroud of Turin

The Shroud of Turin, Italy is a linen cloth measuring fourteen feet, three inches long by three feet, seven inches wide. Historically proclaimed to be the actual burial garment of Jesus, the linen contains a double, head-to-head image of a crucified man reposed in death, which reveals both the obverse and reverse of the body.

With a known history stretching back to at least the fourteenth century, there are a number of important factors which indicate that the shroud is much more ancient, including a number of historical references which extend back several centuries. In the definitive work on the possible history of the shroud, Ian Wilson postulates that the cloth left Palestine about 30 A.D. and proceeded to the ancient kingdom of Edessa, to Constantinople, to France, to Switzerland, and finally to Italy.[14]

In addition to the historical data, there are also a number of scientific reasons which indicate that the shroud should be dated very early. Samples of pollen discovered on the cloth point to an origin in Palestine possibly as far back as the first century, while analyses of the cloth and weave discovered that the shroud is compatible with first century cloth.

However, more important indicators of the age of the shroud have also emerged. Some researchers have asserted that sophisticated methods such as photographic enhancement and computer analysis are able to identify one of the coins placed over the eyes of the man in the shroud as a lepton of Pontius Pilate, minted between 29-32 A.D. Such an identification would be a crucial determination of age.[15]

Biblical questions concerning the type of burial depicted on the shroud have not only failed to discover any discrepancies with the New Testament texts, but have even served to vindicate the cloth. Wrapping a body lengthwise and positioning it as shown on the shroud is corroborated by both recently discovered Qumran burial practices and by the *Code of Jewish Law*, "Laws of Mourning" (chapter 364). Further studies have revealed that the head napkin was first rolled up and then wrapped around the head, as reported by the Gospel of John (11:44; 20:5-7), the Jewish Mishnah (Shabbath 23:5) and the "Laws of Mourning" (chapters 351-352).

While some believe that the body of the man wrapped in the shroud was not washed, the "Laws of Mourning" point out that there are conditions when such washing is not appropriate, such as when a person suffers capital punishment or a violent death. The use of several strips of linen in John is also confirmed on the shroud, since pieces of linen were used there, as well.

One additional point concerns Jesus' burial, which is recorded in the Gospels. Since it is related that Jesus underwent a hasty burial with the women planning to return later to finish the process (Luke 23:54—24:4; Mark 15:42; 16:1-3), we have another explanation here of possible "oddities" in his burial procedure.[16]

One characteristic of the Shroud of Turin which separates it from other such religious remains is that it was the subject of an intense (and ongoing) scientific investigation. In October, 1978, a team of well-qualified scientists applied a large battery of non-destructive tests to the shroud.[17] The research still continues on the data which was gathered. The three most important issues to be answered concerned the nature of the apparent bloodstains, the composition of the image and its cause. In particular, it was determined that the bloodstains were composed of real blood and that the shroud was probably not a fake. The image was not caused by paint, dye, powder or any other foreign substance being added to the cloth. The image on the shroud is composed of oxidized, dehydrated and conjugated fibrils of cloth, similar to the effects of a scorch, but an exact cause of the image was not proven. Additional characteristics of the image, such as its three-dimensional, superficial and non-directional nature, have become quite an enigma to the scientists.[18]

The description of the man who was apparently buried in the shroud has also been enlightening. The scientific team pathologist and other medical doctors determined that the man was crucified and was dead, with his body in a state of rigor mortis. The more the wounds were studied, the more it became obvious that this man's injuries were the same as the gospel reports of Jesus' crucifixion. The most interesting facet of this study is that many unnatural things were done to Jesus and these same things appeared on the shroud.

Both men suffered a series of punctures throughout the scalp from many sharp objects, a seriously bruised face, a horrible whipping (over 100 wounds from this beating have been counted on the shroud), abrasions on both shoulders from a rough, heavy object, and contusions on both knees. Both men had the more normal wounds associated with crucifixion; namely, punctured feet and wrists. Strangely, both men escaped having their ankles broken, as was normal, but both had post-mortem chest wounds instead, from which blood and watery fluid flowed. Both men were buried hastily in fine linen and were buried individually.[19]

Strong indications that the man buried in the shroud is Jesus comes from the correspondence between the two. They agree even down to the small details in about one dozen areas which were not normal crucifixion procedures. The chances are quite minimal that two men would have so many agreements, especially in points of abnormal circumstances. Also, no areas of contradiction apparently exist. It should additionally be remembered that the shroud has been kept for hundreds of years as the actual burial garment of Jesus, long before such scientific testing could be done. While this last point by no means demonstrates the shroud's authenticity in any sense, it does show further a possible relationship between Jesus and the man buried in the shroud.[20]

Naturalistic attempts to account for such phenomena as the three-dimensional, superficial and non-directional image, plus additional details such as its resolute and unsaturated nature, have failed to produce a viable alternative theory which explains all of the data. The scientists reported that they were unable thus far to discover any known natural causes which could account for the shroud's image. In scientific terms, the image is a "mystery."[21]

Perhaps even more amazing, the shroud contains no bodily decomposition, which indicates that the body exited the cloth after a comparatively short interment. Furthermore, according to the scientific team pathologist, the body was probably not unwrapped, as indicated by the fact that many of the bloodstains are intact (including the blood clots), since such action would have disturbed the bloodstains. Even more interesting is our conclusion that the image was caused by some sort of a light or heat scorch which emanated from a dead body in the state of rigor mortis.[22] In short, the converging scientific facts certainly reveal that the body left the cloth by some as yet unknown and mysterious means. Since the man buried in the shroud is probably Jesus, as indicated by the facts, we then have some strong empirical evidence for his resurrection.

It is still possible that the shroud is a fake of some sort or that it is an actual burial garment but did not belong to Jesus. Certainly no absolute proof is available at present. Yet, there is much evidence (including much which cannot be presented here) that the shroud is not a fake, that it quite probably belonged to Jesus and that it provides some strong evidence for his resurrection.[23]

From the Shroud of Turin we may gather a few additional facts concerning Jesus, most of which do not depend on the identification of the man buried in the shroud. (1) Once again we learn of the normal wounds associated with crucifixion such as the pierced wrists and feet, as well as lesser details like the knee contusions (presumably from falling) and the shoulder abrasions (perhaps from carrying part of the cross). (2) We also learn of several abnormal points of crucifixion procedure which this man had in common with Jesus. Such include: the beating, the serious whipping, the scalp wounds caused by sharp objects, the absence of broken ankles, the post-mortem chest wound, and the flow of blood and watery fluid. Afterward, an individual but hasty burial in fine linen for one convicted as a "criminal" is also rather odd.

(3) As with Yohanan, there is strong evidence that the man in the shroud also had to move up and down in order to breathe. The blood from each wrist proceeded down each arm and formed a V-shaped blood flow, which is one evidence that suggests that two major bodily positions were taken on the cross. (4) There is evidence that the man buried in the shroud was raised from the dead, such as the absence of decomposition, an apparent lack of unwrapping the body and a probable scorch from a dead body. If the man in the shroud is Jesus, as indicated by the similarities in dissimilar areas pointed out in (2), then (4) becomes evidence for Jesus' resurrection.

E. Other archaeological data

A few additional finds bear on the historicity of Jesus, if only indirectly. The existence of the pools of Bethesda and Siloam "can be identified with certainty" due to archaeological discoveries.[24] Although the very existence of these two pools does not prove anything in Jesus' life, it is still interesting that the gospel of John associates one of Jesus' healing miracles with each site (John 5:1-9; 9:1-41).

One other note concerns the historical existence of Pontius Pilate. It was mentioned earlier that coins minted by Pilate may have been placed over the eyes of the man buried in the shroud. More examples of these coins have been discovered, minted to honor Pilate's rule and dated 30-31 A.D.[25] Additionally, an inscription containing his name was discovered at Caesarea.[26] Again, this does not prove anything specifically concerning Jesus. However, the historical connection between Pilate and the crucifixion of Jesus is well established by such ancient historians as Tacitus and Josephus.[27]

F. Synopsis of archaeological sources

From these archaeological sources we learn numerous facts which are beneficial in a study of Christ's life, especially with regard to his death and resurrection. By their very nature, these facts derived from archaeology often tend to be verifiable and hence produce a firm basis for history.

Concerning the taxation-census reported in Luke 2, data from archaeological discoveries reveal several facts. Such processes were fairly common in the ancient Roman Empire, involving persons traveling to their own cities. This taxation-census began during Augustus' reign (37 B.C.—14 A.D.) and continued to the third century A.D., often at fourteen year intervals. One such taxation-census was apparently enacted at approximately the same time as Jesus' birth.

With regard to crucifixion, we learn that victims had their wrists and feet nailed to the cross (Yohanan, shroud), and were apparently made to carry part of the cross to the crucifixion site, which often resulted in falls (shroud). Normal crucifixion procedure usually involved breaking the victim's legs (Yohanan). That the shroud is probably Jesus' and that its contents then apply directly to him is indicated by numerous agreements in points of abnormal crucifixion procedure, such as the crown of thorns, the severe beating and whipping, the absence of broken ankles, the post-mortem chest wound and the flow of blood and watery fluid. Other "odd" similarities in the burial include an individual burial for a crucified person, yet a hasty burial in fine linen. We also learn much about medical factors, such as the cause of death being closely related to asphyxiation, as the victim pushed up and down in order to breathe (Yohanan, shroud).

The Jewish burial process often involved a sealed tomb (Nazareth Decree). There were apparently reports in Palestine which caused the emperor to issue a warning against grave robbing, which was punishable by death (Nazareth Decree). We also have possible evidence for Jesus' resurrection, which is implied in the need for the emperor to levy such a strong punishment in Palestine for grave robbing, since the report of the resurrection had already saturated the Empire (Nazareth Decree). As we saw in Chapter III, the fraud (or stolen body) theory is decisively disproven by the facts.

Strong evidence for the resurrection is also derived from the information on the shroud. In particular, the lack of bodily decomposition, indicative of a rather hasty bodily departure, the apparent lack of unwrapping and the probable presence of an image caused by a scorch from a dead body, all reveal the probability of Jesus' resurrection.

G. Conclusion

While the archaeological evidence for the life of Jesus numerically includes only a comparatively few examples, these instances are of high quality when speaking of corroboration especially for Jesus' death and resurrection. The skeleton of Yohanan is quite valuable in relating more of the exact nature of crucifixion, including both the mechanics of the process and a number of relevant medical factors. The Nazareth Decree provides some details concerning Jewish burial and hints about Jesus' resurrection. The Shroud of Turin is an excellent witness to most of the details involved in the processes of crucifixion and burial. When identified as probably being the burial garment of Jesus, these facts of crucifixion and burial apply directly to him. Additionally, the shroud supplies probable evidence for the resurrection.[28]

[1]See Bruce, *Christian Origins*, p. 192, for example.

[2]Ibid., pp. 193-194.

[3]Ibid., p. 194.

[4]Robert Boyd, *Tells, Tombs, and Treasure* (Grand Rapids: Baker Book House, 1969), p. 175.

[5]Cf. Bruce, *Christian Origins*, pp. 193-194 with Boyd, ibid., p. 175. Bruce prefers the date 10-9 B.C. for the empire-wide census, with that which took place in Judea occurring a few years later. Boyd places the date of the earlier census at 6-5 B.C., which coincides closely with accepted dates for Jesus' birth.

[6]Bruce, *Christian Origins*, p. 192.

[7]Vasilius Tzaferis, "Jewish Tombs At and Near Giv'at ha-Mivtar," *Israel Exploration Journal* 20 (1970), pp. 38-59.

[8]Nica Haas, "Anthropological Observations on the Skeletal Remains from Giv'at ha-Mivtar," *Israel Exploration Journal* 20 (1970), cited in Maier, *First Easter* (New York: Harper and Row, Publishers, 1973), pp. 78-80.

[9]Tacitus, *Annals*, 15.44.

[10]See Maier, p. 119.

[11]Ibid., pp. 119-120.

[12]Suetonius, *Claudius*, 25; cf. Acts 18:2.

[13]See Bruce, *Christian Origins*, p. 196; Maier, pp. 119-120; Boyd, p. 185.

[14]See Ian Wilson, *The Shroud of Turin* (New York: Doubleday and Company, Inc., 1978).

[15]For these details, see Kenneth E. Stevenson and Gary R. Habermas, *Verdict on the Shroud* (Ann Arbor: Servant Books, 1981), especially Chapter 2.

[16]Ibid., Chapter 4.

[17]For an authoritative description of some of the proposed tests to be performed on the shroud, see Kenneth E. Stevenson, Editor, *Proceedings of the 1977 United States Conference on the Shroud of Turin* (Bronx: Holy Shroud Guild, 1977).

[18]See Stevenson and Habermas, Chapters 5-6. See also John Heller, *Report on the Shroud of Turin* (Boston: Houghton Mifflin Company, 1983), especially Chapters 12-14.

[19]Stevenson and Habermas, Chapters 3, 10.

[20]For details concerning this correspondence that cannot be presented in this book, see chapter 9, where a study in probability is conducted.

[21]Heller, p. 218.

[22]These are the conclusions of Ken Stevenson and myself and do not necessarily represent the views of any other researchers. See Stevenson and Habermas, Chapter 11. For a more detailed and intricate argument concerning the shroud as evidence for the resurrection, see also Gary R. Habermas, "The Shroud of

Turin: A Rejoinder to Basinger and Basinger," *Journal of the Evangelical Theological Society* 25 (1982), pp. 219-227.

[23]A stern disclaimer is definitely in order here. Whether the shroud is or is not the true burial sheet of Jesus, it is absolutely crucial that we not be involved with any sort of worship or veneration of this cloth. God's warning against worshipping *any* object still stands, along with the serious judgment pronounced against those who disobey (Exod. 20:4-6, for example). Stevenson and I wish it to be clear that we totally oppose any such activities.

[24]Bruce, *Christian Origins*, p. 188.

[25]Boyd, p. 183

[26]Ibid.

[27]Tacitus, *Annals*, 15.44; Josephus, *Antiquities*, 18:3.

[28]It is true, however, that the gospel accounts are needed in order to *identify* the man in the shroud as Jesus, according to probability. Not only have these gospel sources been shown to be accurate and trustworthy (see Chapters II-III), but even apart from them, the shroud gives exceptionally strong evidence for crucifixion and burial in general, as well as for the resurrection of "some person." (See Habermas, "The Shroud of Turin: A Rejoinder to Basinger and Basinger" for further details here.)

8

Summary and Assessment

Having finished our treatment of the ancient pre- and non-New Testament sources for Jesus' life, we turn now to a final assessment of this material.[1] Our first interest is to present an integrated summary of the historical reports concerning Jesus' life, death and resurrection. Lastly, we will present our final evaluation of the strength of these sources in establishing these facts.

A. Synopsis of sources

Many aspects of Jesus' life have been reported by the four categories of evidence which we have examined in Part Two. Our ancient material from non-Christian, creedal (plus critical), non-New Testament Christian and archaeological sources presents quite a detailed look at the career of Jesus. We will begin this chapter by summarizing all of the reports from these four areas, which will be advantageous for a complete view of this data.

The Life and Person of Jesus. It is reported (1) that Jesus really did become a man (Barnabas; creeds: Phil. 2:6ff.; 1 John 4:2) and (2) lived on the earth in human history (Ignatius). (3) He came from the tribe of Judah (Justin) and (4) was of the lineage of Jesse and David (Justin; Ignatius; creed: 2 Tim. 2:8).

Archaeological discoveries have shown that, before Jesus' birth, (5) a taxation was proclaimed by the Roman authorities, (6) who required that people travel back to their home cities. (7) Required nearly every fourteen years, just such a taxation apparently occurred at approximately the same time as Jesus' birth.

(8) Jesus was born of Mary (Ignatius), (9) who was a virgin (Ignatius; Justin), and (10) he had a brother named James (Josephus). (11) Jesus was born in the city of Bethlehem, which was located about five miles from Jerusalem and it is recorded (12) that his birth could he verified by the

records of Cyrenius, who was the first procurator of Judea (Justin). (13) Later, Jesus was visited by Arabian Magi, who had first visited Herod (Justin).

With regard to his public ministry, Jesus (14) was baptised by John (Ignatius; creed: Rom. 10:9-10) and (15) chose his apostles (Barnabas; Justin). Geographically, (16) Jesus' ministry was centered in Palestine (Tacitus; Lucian; Acts of Pilate). (17) He was known as a wise, virtuous and ethical man (Josephus, Mara Bar-Serapion). (18) As the result of his ministry and preaching (creed: 1 Tim. 3:16), (19) he made many disciples from both the Jews and the Gentiles (Josephus; Talmud; creed: 1 Tim. 3:16).

We are told (20) that Jesus performed miracles (Acts of Pilate; Quadratus; Barnabas; Justin). It is reported (21) that some people were healed and others were raised from the dead and (22) that some of the eyewitnesses of these occurrences were still alive (Quadratus). It is also claimed (23) that Pilate filed a report with the Roman officials which corroborated these details (Justin). Additionally, Jesus both (24) fulfilled Old Testament prophecy, thereby validating his claims (Justin; cf. Josephus) and (25) made prophecies himself which were later fulfilled (Phlegon), (26) such as his own resurrection (Justin).

Many of the sources which we investigated comment on the person of Jesus.[2] (27) We are told that on one occasion Jesus asked his disciples who they believed that he was (Gospel of Thomas). Various answers are given in the gnostic works, all of which agree (28) that he was both God and man. While he was a real flesh and blood person (Gospel of Truth, Treatise on Resurrection), as indicated (in the context) by the title Son of Man (Gospel of Thomas), he is also called the Son of God (Treatise on Resurrection, Gospel of Truth) and the "All" (Gospel of Thomas).

The pre-New Testament creeds are also in agreement that Jesus was deity. We are told that Jesus was of the same nature or essence as God (creed: Phil. 2:6). He is given the titles of Lord (creeds: 1 Cor. 11:23; Rom. 1:4; Rom. 10:9; Luke 24:34), Son (creed: Rom. 1:3-4) and Christ (creeds: 1 Cor. 15:3; Rom. 1:4; 1 Tim. 6:13; 2 Tim. 2:8; 1 Pet. 3:18; 1 John 4:2).

Secular sources report similar data. (29) Jesus was worshipped as deity (Pliny; Lucian), (30) some believed that he was the Messiah (Josephus) and, accordingly, (31) called him "King" (Mara Bar-Serapion).

The Teachings of Jesus. It is recorded (32) that Jesus preached to and taught Israel, a people whom he loved (Barnabas). (33) He exhorted the

Jews to repent, yet they refused to do so even after he rose from the dead (Justin).

(34) Jesus' major teaching was the gospel (cf. 1 Cor. 15:1-4), (35) which he received from God and later imparted to his apostles (Clement; Barnabas). (36) It is asserted that the apostles were fully convinced of the truthfulness of the gospel and that they, in turn, preached the Kingdom of God everywhere (Clement).

The tendency among some of the secular sources was (37) to view Jesus as a philosopher with some distinct teachings (Lucian; Mara Bar-Serapion; cf. Gospel of Thomas). For instance, Lucian refers to Jesus as a "sage." Lucian and Pliny, in particular, corroborate some of the major teachings of Jesus as mentioned earlier in the Christian sources.

Lucian asserts (38) that Jesus introduced new teachings in Palestine. These included (39) the need for conversion, (40) the denial of the gods and (41) the brotherhood of all believers. Jesus' teachings additionally included and encouraged (42) worship of himself, (43) living according to his teachings, (44) the importance of faith and (45) immortality, which led to a contempt for death among believers. Lucian also notes (46) that Christians had sacred Scripture which was frequently read.

In addition to the point mentioned earlier, that Jesus was worshipped by early believers as deity, Pliny also reports (47) an oath taken by believers not to commit sin, which reflects Jesus' ethical teachings. Additionally, Pliny tells us (48) that true believers could not be enticed or forced to worship the gods, and (49) that they worshipped on a certain day of the week before dawn, both which reflect Jesus' teachings.

Lastly, the Gospel of Truth adds (50) that Jesus taught his listeners about his Father and (51) that Jesus realized his death was the basis for the life of many people.

The Death of Jesus. From the early creed in 1 Cor. 11:23ff. we learn (52) that Jesus attended a dinner (53) on the evening on which he was betrayed. At this meal he (54) gave thanks for the food, and (55) shared both bread and drink, (56) which he referred to as the sacrifice of his body and blood for sin.

(57) The Jewish leaders determined that Jesus was guilty of teaching spiritual heresy and of leading Israel to apostasy (Talmud; cf. Apocryphon of John). (58) As a result, the Jews sent out a herald who proclaimed that Jesus would be stoned for his teachings, though anyone who wished was invited to defend him. However, no one came forward to speak for him (Talmud).

Jesus (59) appeared before Pilate and (60) made a good confession (creed: 1 Tim. 6:13), which may have been an affirmation of his messiahship. (61) After being persecuted (Gospel of Truth) and (62) as a result of his teachings (Lucian), (63) Jesus was put to death (Gospel of Thomas; Treatise on Resurrection; creeds: 1 Cor. 15:3; 1 Pet. 3:18; Rom. 4:25; 1 Tim. 2:6). He died (64) at the hands of Roman procurator Pontius Pilate (Talmud; Ignatius), (65) during the local rule of Herod (Ignatius). (66) So Jesus was crucified (Josephus; Talmud; Lucian; Gospel of Truth; Acts of Pilate; Ignatius; Barnabas; Justin; creed: Phil 2:6f.) (67) during the reign of Roman Emperor Tiberius (Tacitus).

Even some details of Jesus' crucifixion are provided by these sources. (68) The event reportedly occurred on Passover Eve (Talmud). Victims of crucifixion, such as Jesus, (69) were apparently made to carry their cross (or part of it) to the crucifixion site, which often resulted in falls (Shroud of Turin), followed by (70) these persons having their wrists and feet nailed to the cross (Yohanan; shroud; Tacitus; Gospel of Truth; Acts of Pilate; Ignatius; Justin). (71) Normal crucifixion additionally involved breaking the victim's legs in order to hasten death by asphyxiation (Yohanan), (72) which is the normal cause of death in crucifixion, as revealed by the need for the person to push up and down in order to breathe (Yohanan; Shroud of Turin).

Since the Shroud of Turin is probably Jesus',[3] it confirms numerous details of his crucifixion at points which involved uncommon procedures,[4] such as (73) the crown of thorns, (74) the severe beating and bodily whipping, (75) the absence of any broken ankles, (76) the post-mortem chest wound and (77) the blood and watery fluid flowing from the wound.

While the crucifixion was in progress, (78) Jesus' executioners gambled for his garments (Acts of Pilate; Justin). (79) Mara Bar-Serapion asserted that Jesus was executed unjustly and that, as a result, the Jews were judged by God. (80) The creed in 1 Pet. 3:18 also notes the contrast between a righteous person dying for sinners. It is related (81) that Jesus was on the cross until evening, (82) after which his body was removed and he was buried (Justin; creed: 1 Cor. 15:4).

The man buried in the Shroud of Turin was also buried (83) hastily, (84) individually and (85) in fine linen, which are all uncommon procedures for a crucifixion victim, further linking this cloth with Jesus. Furthermore, (86) Jewish burial procedure often involved sealing the tomb (Nazareth Decree). Interestingly, (87) grave robbing was punishable by death in Palestine (Nazareth Decree).

The Resurrection of Jesus. (88) During this time Jesus' friends left and denied him (Justin), experiencing despair at his death. (89) Then, three days after Jesus' death, the tomb in which he was buried was found empty (Justin; creed: 1 Cor. 15:4, implied; cf. Toledoth Jesu). (90) The Jews claimed that the disciples stole the body and proclaimed him risen (Toledoth Jesu; Justin), but such a view fails to explain the known facts.[5]

Numerous sources assert (91) that Jesus was raised from the dead (creeds: Luke 24:34; 2 Tim. 2:8; Clement; Ignatius; Justin; Gospel of Truth; Gospel of Thomas; Treatise on Resurrection). Strong evidence for the resurrection comes from the (92) early reports of this event, probably dating from the 30s A.D., and (93) from the eyewitnesses themselves, who reported having seen the risen Jesus personally (creeds: 1 Cor. 15:3ff.; Luke 24:34).

Additional reports indicated (94) that Jesus appeared to Peter and the other disciples (creed: 1 Cor. 15:5; Josephus; Ignatius; Justin). (95) Jesus invited them to touch his body, which they did (Ignatius), (96) and he even ate and drank in their presence (Ignatius). (97) During this time, Jesus also taught his disciples concerning the Old Testament prophecy which he had fulfilled (Justin). An interesting facet concerning Jesus' resurrection is that he did not appear only to believers. For instance, he was seen by two of the best known skeptics in the early church—(98) James, the brother of Jesus and (99) Paul (creed: 1 Cor. 15:7-9).

The Shroud of Turin adds further facts to the claim that Jesus was raised from the dead. (100) There is no decomposition on the shroud, which indicates a hasty bodily departure. Also, (101) the body buried in the cloth was apparently not unwrapped, while (102) the probable cause of the image on the shroud is a scorch from a dead body.

It is asserted that after Jesus' resurrection and his subsequent brief ministry on earth, (103) he ascended to heaven (creeds: 1 Tim. 3:16; Phil. 2:6f.; Justin; cf. Quadratus) and (104) was exalted (Apocryphon of John; Gospel of Thomas).

As a result of these events (105) Jesus' disciples were transformed from persons who were afraid to be associated with him just a short time before to strong witnesses whose lives were changed (Tacitus; Suetonius; Mara Bar-Serapion; Josephus; Clement; cf. Pliny; cf. creed: 1 Tim. 3:16). (106) The gospel became the center of early Christian preaching (creed: 1 Cor. 15:1-4; Clement). (107) The resurrection of Jesus was viewed as the validation of his claims (creeds: Rom. 1:3-4; 10:9-10; Clement; Ignatius). (108) Early Christian preaching took place in Jerusalem, where Jesus had been crucified shortly before. (109) The church began and grew, (110) with Sunday as the primary day of worship (cf. Pliny; Barnabas).

B. Evaluation of sources

The Life and Person of Jesus. We have examined a total of thirty-nine ancient sources for the life of Jesus, which include seventeen non-Christian, thirteen early creedal, five non-New Testament Christian and four archaeological sources. From this data we have enumerated 110 reported facts concerning the life, teachings, crucifixion and resurrection of Jesus. This is not to say that all of these sources are of the same quality (for a variety of reasons). But these facts (and those mentioned below) are spread out across all of the categories and types of writers and are thus rather evenly balanced.

There can be little doubt that this is a substantial amount of pre- and non-New Testament material for Jesus' existence and for numerous facts about his life. In light of these reports we can perceive all the more how groundless the speculations are which deny his existence or which postulate only a minimal amount of facts concerning him. Much of ancient history is based on many fewer sources which are much later than the events which they record, as pointed out earlier. While some believe that we know almost nothing about Jesus from ancient, non-New Testament sources, this plainly is not the case. Not only are there many such sources, but Jesus is one of the persons of ancient history concerning whom we have a significant amount of quality data. His is one of the most mentioned and most substantiated lives in ancient times.

We should also briefly mention the historical fact that the deity of Jesus was widely reported in the ancient writings which we investigated. Of our thirty-nine sources, twenty-four record this teaching, which surprisingly includes seven of the seventeen secular sources. It was pointed out in Chapter III that Jesus claimed to be deity. The pre-New Testament creeds, in particular, provide additional corroborative evidence for this since they follow so soon after Jesus' ministry. These creeds reveal that the church did not simply teach Jesus' deity a generation later, as is so often repeated in contemporary theology, because this doctrine is definitely present in the earliest church. The best explanation for these creeds is that they properly represent Jesus' own teachings, especially since he made similar claims.

The Crucifixion of Jesus. Of all the events in Jesus' life, more ancient sources specifically mention his death than any other single occurrence. Of the thirty-nine ancient sources, twenty-two relate this fact, often with details. Eleven of these sources are non-Christian,[6] which exhibits an incredible amount of interest in this event.

Not only is Jesus' death by crucifixion of major concern to these authors, but eight of the twenty-two sources give various details about the crucifixion, from political information concerning the current rulers, to historical specifications of the times in which Jesus died, to religious details about the reason for his death. Perhaps most important, however, are the sources which give medical information from the actual details of crucifixion to the cause of death in such instances.

It is especially these sources which give medical details which provide refutations of the swoon theory and reveal that Jesus was indeed dead due to the rigors of crucifixion.[7] This theory was rejected by critical scholars at the end of the nineteenth century,[8] and is still rejected today because it is refuted by the facts.[9] Therefore, the facts which witness to Jesus' death by crucifixion establish both the reality of the event itself, as well as numerous details surrounding it. It is fair to assert that this is one of the best attested facts in ancient history. After Jesus' death, he was buried. This fact is not only strongly confirmed by five different sources,[10] but is generally a normal consequence of dying.

The Resurrection of Jesus. At this point in our evaluation we arrive at the crucial issue which brings us face to face with a miracle-claim. Again, it is not our purpose in this volume to make a judgment as to whether the resurrection is an actual miracle, but to evaluate whether it was an actual historical event. Concerning this issue an examination of the details provides us with an affirmative answer—the facts prove Jesus' resurrection from the dead.

Of our thirty-nine sources, thirteen specifically record the resurrection, while an additional ten more provide relevant facts surrounding this occurrence. Even if we were only to use the known facts which are accepted as historical by critical scholars, we still arrive at four major categories of evidence for the resurrection of Jesus.

First, alternative theories which have been hypothesized by critics to explain the resurrection on naturalistic grounds have failed to explain the data and are refuted by the facts. Combinations of these theories also fail on these grounds. This is further illustrated by the refutation of David Hume's thesis concerning miracles (as well as other related approaches), by the nineteenth century individual liberal critiques of each of these naturalistic theories and by the twentieth century rejection of them as a whole.[11] Such a critical rejection of critical theories is a significant development.

Second, even the accepted historical facts alone provide at least nine historical evidences for the resurrection, as pointed out above.[12] In particular, that this event was reported *early* (probably in the 30s A.D.) by the very *eyewitnesses* who attested to seeing the risen Jesus (1 Cor. 15:3ff.) is extremely strong evidence in favor of the literal resurrection.[13] The historical evidence for the empty tomb is also very strong, as are the changed lives of the disciples and the conversions of Paul and James. Therefore, a historical case for this event can be built on both a failure of critical hypotheses on the one hand plus the presence of valid, positive evidences on the other.

Third, even if we were to utilize only the four "core" historical facts which are accepted by virtually all scholars who deal with this issue, we still have a significant basis on which to both refute the naturalistic theories and provide the major evidences for the resurrection. The primary strength of these four facts is that they have been established by critical methodology and thus cannot be rejected by those who have doubts concerning other issues such as Scripture. In other words, the minimum amount of historical facts is sufficient to establish the historicity of Jesus' resurrection. Doubts on other issues do not disturb this basic fact.[14]

Fourth, the Shroud of Turin provides some strong scientific, repeatable evidence for the resurrection, even though there is no proof available at this point.[15] Since the shroud is probably not a fake of any kind but a real archaeological artifact, and since it is quite probably Jesus' burial garment, it contains much important information not only concerning the crucifixion, but also concerning the resurrection. That there is no bodily decomposition reveals that the body exited after a comparatively brief period of time. Additionally, there are signs that the body was probably not unwrapped and that the image on the cloth was probably caused by a scorch from a dead body, which is additional and highly evidential data in favor of Jesus' resurrection.[16]

These four major categories of arguments for the resurrection do not exhaust the ancient evidence for this event,[17] but they do prove this fact as a literal event of history by normal historical methodology. It is the final capstone and fitting conclusion for the unique life, teachings and death of Jesus. And the place that the resurrection might play in Christian theism is a logical sequel for just such a study,[18] for the only time that such a resurrection is ever known to have occurred, it happened to the person who seriously made the most unique claims in the history of religions.

Notes

[1]Our apologetic summary of the so-called debunking efforts is accomplished in Appendix One.

[2]Our explicit intention in Chapter VI was only to mention the post-New Testament Christian sources which reported historical facts during the life of Jesus. We did not mention these sources that also make claims concerning Jesus' deity. For examples, see Clement, *Corinthians*, 36; Ignatius, *Ephesians*, 7, 18; *Romans*, Introduction; *Smyrnaeans*, 1; *To Polycarp*, 8; Polycarp, *Philippians*, 12. In these examples from Ignatius and Polycarp, Jesus is specifically called God.

[3]Even if the Shroud of Turin is not Jesus', it still provides evidence which confirms the crucifixion, since the shroud is very probably not a fake. This means that it is a real burial cloth which apparently wrapped the body of a crucified man.

[4]In fact, as pointed out in Chapter VII, the key to the probable identification of the shroud as the actual burial garment of Jesus is the large number of agreements in points of abnormal crucifixion procedure.

[5]See Chapters IV,H and V,D.

[6]Of the remaining eleven sources which mention the death of Jesus, six are from the creedal, three are from the non-New Testament and two from the archaeological sources.

[7]See Chapter III,C for these refutations.

[8]Riggenbach, *Resurrection of Jesus*, pp. 48-49; Orr, *Resurrection of Jesus*, p. 92.

[9]Barth, *Church Dogmatics*, vol. IV, p. 340; Brown, "The Resurrection and Biblical Criticism," p. 223.

[10]These sources include the early creed in 1 Cor. 15:3ff. and the Shroud of Turin, as well as hostile sources such as the *Toledoth Jesu* and the information implied in the Nazareth decree.

[11]See V,C-D for more details.

[12]See V,C for a list of these evidences which are based on the accepted historical facts.

[13]See V,B in particular.

[14]See V,C-D for details.

[15]Because of the incomplete nature of the shroud studies, the Shroud of Turin could still turn out to be a fake or simply real but just not the actual burial garment of Jesus. Therefore, it is extremely important to point out that the case for

the resurrection not only is independent of this point, but it is very possibly even the weakest of the four categories of evidence. At least category three (the "core facts") is evidentially stronger. Yet the shroud is certainly important to our presentation and the only one of the four categories which presents scientific, repeatable support. We simply do not want the present popularity of the subject to place it out of perspective in our study.

[16]See VII,D.

[17]For instance, the evidence from the Nazareth Decree (VII,C) and the assertions of Tacitus and Suetonius that Jesus' teachings broke out again in Palestine *after* his death are other avenues which might be explored.

[18]See Habermas, *The Resurrection of Jesus: An Apologetic.*

Appendix One:
An Apologetic Outline

In this summary appendix, our major purpose is twofold. First, we will systematize our answers to those who, in Chapters II-III, have attempted to explain away the unique elements in the life of Jesus. In these earlier chapters our presentation was topical and directed more to certain issues and authors rather than to the overall area of study on that particular question. Second, new material from Chapters IV-VII will also be included here when this was not the case in our earlier study.

In order to best facilitate the goal of this chapter, comparatively few notes will be utilized. Instead, reference will be made back to the chapter and section in which this discussion occurred so that the sources can be checked. This material will be organized according to topical, outline form for easier reference and will be systematized in three major categories: the New Testament, Jesus and miracle-claims. We will not be concerned with references back to the original attacks presented in Chapters II-III but only with the positive responses which were made to each of those views. In this way, this chapter will be a tighter unit and will not be disjointed as our earlier responses were because of the constant need to give similar answers to similar issues.

A. The trustworthiness of the New Testament

In spite of the fact that Part Two in this book was chiefly concerned with extra-New Testament sources, the trustworthiness of the New Testament was a recurring thesis in Chapters II-III, where it was necessary to answer certain charges. Accordingly, while our evidence for the life, death and resurrection of Jesus has been almost entirely gleaned from pre- and non-New Testament sources, this section is still needed by virtue of our responses to others.

1. The New Testament has better manuscript evidence that any other ancient book (II,B):
   a. There are over 5,000 New Testament manuscripts and portions of manuscripts. By comparison, many (if not most) classical works have less than 20 manuscripts.
   b. The dates of the New Testament manuscripts are close to the original writings, with one gospel fragment (Ryland's) which dates from about 25 years after the gospel of John and most of the New Testament (Chester Beatty Papyri) from 50-150 years after the originals. Most classical works date from 700-1400 years after the originals.
   c. None of the New Testament is lost or missing. By comparison, 107 of Livy's 142 books of history have been lost and about one-half of Tacitus' 30 books of *Annals* and *Histories* are missing.
2. The gospel accounts of Jesus are based on eyewitness testimony, as recognized by many contemporary scholars (III,E):
   a. The apostle Matthew is often taken by numerous critical scholars as either the author or the major source behind the first gospel.
   b. It is usually recognized that Peter is the major source for Mark's gospel.
   c. Not only is the Lukan authorship of the third gospel and Acts well supported, but his reliance on eyewitness sources (Luke 1:1-4), and his companionship with Paul are also well recognized.
   d. The fourth gospel, once considered the most unreliable of the Gospels, has once again been recognized by a number of critical scholars as being based on the eyewitness testimony of John.
3. The Gospels are very close to the events which they record, with three out of four being dated within one generation and all four within seventy years after Jesus' life, all during the lives of eyewitnesses (III,E).
4. The Gospels are trustworthy sources, as explained by A. M. Hunter (III,E):
   a. These Christian authors, like their Jewish counterparts, were careful to preserve traditional material.
   b. The Gospels are close to eyewitness sources.
   c. The gospel authors were honest reporters.
   d. The picture of Jesus presented in the four Gospels is virtually the same.[1]

5. The Gospels and Acts exhibit a specific interest in reporting histori-cal facts, not mythology. When judged by normal historical stan-dards, the New Testament "measures up" well. This is especially the case when the life of Jesus is reported (II,A-B).[2]

6. Even historians of antiquity oppose the application of radical form criticism to New Testament studies. According to A. N. Sherwin-White and Michael Grant, radical form criticism fails at a number of crucial points (II,B):[3]

   a. Numerous ancient works exhibit similar intentions and metho-dologies to that of the New Testament authors, and yet these an-cient works are well accepted as historical works.

   b. There are no such ancient works in the category that form critics place the Gospels.

   c. The Gospels are much closer to the events that they describe than numerous events recorded in ancient histories, which sometimes occurred hundreds of years before they were reported.

   d. Some ancient histories disagree with each other very strongly, and yet much history is ascertained from these works.

   e. Form critics often ignore the causes for the experiences of the earliest apostles while historians of antiquity attempt to ascer-tain just such causes.

   f. New Testament portions, such as Acts, have been confirmed by external tests of historicity.

   g. Even if form criticism is applied to the Gospels, this does not preclude the ascertaining of much historical material contained in them.

7. Older studies that attempt to discern numerous Hellenistic influ-ences on the New Testament authors are somewhat outdated, with much attention at present being focused on the Jewish backgrounds of these books (II,B).

8. Older attempts to date the Gospels later, often into the second cen-tury A.D., are no longer well received by critical scholars. Such ef-forts would be convenient for certain liberal theories, but are disproven by the facts (II,A).

9. The Gospels were recognized as inspired books almost immediately after being written (III,E):

   a. 1 Tim. 5:18 quotes Luke 10:7 and refers to it as "Scripture."

   b. Clement of Rome (about 95 A.D.) speaks of the "Gospel" and quotes portions found in all three synoptic Gospels, referring to them as the words of Jesus (Corinthians 13,46).

c. Ignatius (Smyrnaeans 3; ca. 110 A.D.) and Polycarp (Philippians 2,7; ca. 115 A.D.) both refer to verses in the synoptic Gospels as the words of Christ.

d. The Didache (8, 15-16; ca. late first or early second century) refers to the "Gospels" twice and quotes portions found in all three synotic Gospels each time.

e. Barnabas (ca. 135 A.D.) refers to Matt. 22:14 as "Scripture" (4) and quotes a portion found in all three synoptics as the apostles' "Gospel" (5).

f. Papias' fragments (Exposition of Oracles of the Lord; ca. 140 A.D.) assert that the Gospels of Matthew, Mark and John are all based on eyewitness testimony (III, XIX, XX). Luke was not questioned, but Papias' portion on the third Gospel is simply missing.

10. Paul's epistles were also recognized as inspired Scripture almost immediately after being written (III,E):

a. 2 Pet. 3:15-16 calls Paul's epistles "Scripture."

b. Clement of Rome (Corinthians 47), Ignatius (Ephesians 10; To Polycarp 5) and Polycarp (Philippians 1, 3-4. 6) all refer to Paul's writings as inspired.

B. The historicity of Jesus

1. The trustworthy Gospels (Section A above) exhibit much interest in the historical Jesus and give accurate accounts of his life, death and resurrection (II,A).

2. Numerous pre- and extra-biblical sources record much ancient testimony concerning Jesus within 125 years after Jesus' death (IV-VII):

a. Secular historians, government officials, religious records, etc. report many details about Jesus from non-Christian viewpoints (IV).

b. Early Christian creeds, which pre-date the New Testament and the historical facts which virtually all critical scholars admit, provide an extremely strong case for the death and resurrection of Jesus (V).

c. Ancient Christian sources preserve a number of historical statements about Jesus (VI).

d. Archaeology contributes several finds which illuminate and provide evidence especially for the death and resurrection of Jesus (VII).

3. In spite of the excellent pre- and extra-biblical evidence for the his-

toricity of Jesus, there are also good reasons why there are not even more such sources (II,D).

4. To reject Jesus' miracles *a priori* is to claim an omniscient viewpoint and to ignore correct inductive procedure where all facts are investigated before a decision is made (I,C; II,B-C; Section C below).

5. To reject Jesus' doctrinal teachings *a priori* as valid for today is to pick and choose portions of the Gospels. Further, if Jesus was raised from the dead, there is, at a minimum, some implied significance for Jesus' teachings as well (II,C).

6. Without a significant historical basis in the life of Jesus, Christianity would have no impetus for its beginning. This has led to a significant critique of Bultmann by his own students. Some have blamed Bultmann and others with twentieth century gnosticism at this point (II,B).

7. The ancient mystery religions provide no inspiration for early Christians, for several reasons (II,A):

   a. The *early* testimony of creeds such as 1 Cor. 15:3ff. and Luke 24:34 reveal that the crucial facts of the gospel were reported before there was any time for legends to arise.

   b. More importantly on this issue, the *eyewitness* testimony of 1 Cor. 15:3ff. and other portions links the gospel testimony to the *original persons* actually involved and not to any legendary mythology.

   c. There is no clear and early evidence for a resurrection occurring in a mystery religion before the late second century A.D.

   d. There are numerous differences between Jesus and the mystery religions.

   e. The mystery religions had very little influence in Palestine.

   f. The trustworthy Gospels give an historically accurate portrayal of Jesus.

8. Jesus did die on the cross, as indicated by several facts (III,C):

   a. David Strauss' famous critique showed that even if the swoon theory was true, it could not have accounted for the resurrection faith of the disciples.[4]

   b. The nature of crucifixion, including the discovery of Yohanan's skeleton, relates both the nature and surety of death by this method.

   c. The nature of Jesus' heart wound indicates that it would have killed him if he had still been alive.

178

    d. The Shroud of Turin presents very strong evidence for Jesus' death.

    e. The trustworthy Gospels give accurate accounts of Jesus' death.

9. There are numerous differences between Jesus' teachings and those of the Qumran community and between Jesus and the Essene Teacher of Righteousness (see III,D for lists). More important, linking Jesus to the Qumran community would not necessarily be detrimental to Christianity at all (III,D).

10. Jesus' message was not changed by his followers or by Paul, in particular (III,F):

    a. Jesus claimed to be deity in the synoptics as well as in John. Often this was done by his words, such as his claims to be Son of God, Son of Man and Messiah.[5] At other times he showed his deity by his actions, such as forgiving sin, fulfilling Old Testament messianic prophecy and by claiming authority much greater than that of the Jewish leaders.[6]

    b. Numerous pre-Pauline creeds such as Phil. 2:6-11, Rom. 1:3-4 and 1 Cor. 11:23ff. teach the full deity of Jesus, which further reveals that this doctrine definitely does not originate with Paul.

    c. Paul also taught the deity of Jesus,[7] so there is no conflict with the Gospels.

    d. Neither Jesus nor Paul taught that Christianity was a new religion. Both held that Christianity was a fulfillment of Judaism.[8]

    e. Jesus' central teaching of the Kingdom of God and its entrance requirements of faith in his person and teachings is found in all four Gospels[9] and in Paul's epistles.[10]

    f. Paul was known as the apostle to the Gentiles.[11] Not only did Jesus command his disciples to take the gospel to the Gentiles,[12] but this was actually a fulfillment of Old Testament prophecy, not a new doctrine.[13]

    g. The fact that Paul's message was checked and approved by the original apostles (Gal. 2:1-10) reveals that he was not teaching a message contrary to Jesus'. Such official apostolic recognition was not only given to Paul's original message but also to his epistles, which were written later and immediately recognized as Scripture (2 Pet. 3:15-16; Clement of Rome; Ignatius and Polycarp; see A,10 above).

    h. Such an approach to the New Testament usually involves picking and choosing certain texts while ignoring others.

    i. The trustworthiness of the New Testament insures theological continuity.

    j. Since Jesus literally rose from the dead, any verification of the truthfulness of his teachings would even extend to Paul's message and writings, since they are in agreement, as just pointed out.

11. Jesus was not an international traveller after his life and near death in Palestine (III,G):

    a. There is no real historical evidence for such international ventures.

    b. The swoon theory fails and is rejected by all critical scholars (see Section B,8 above).

    c. These endeavors almost always involve a long trail of illogic and incredibly mysterious connections.

    d. The trustworthy Gospels refute these theses.

C. Miracle-claims

1. No event can be rejected *a priori* unless one assumes an omniscient viewpoint. Since this is impossible, the facts must be examined (I,C; II,C).

2. The laws of nature do not disallow any events, but are simply descriptions of the ways in which things usually occur. Hume was incorrect in endeavoring to utilize man's experience of these laws against the existence of miracles (see I,C; V,D).

3. Twentieth century science has changed, and while it certainly does not prove miracles, neither does it disallow them (I,C).

4. Correct inductive research methodology demands a systematic investigation of all relevant data before a decision is made. Such a process is observed in science, medicine, law, and journalism, as well as history. In a similar way, miracle-claims must also be checked out before a philosophical or historical judgment is made (I,C; II,C).

5. Although many would place miracle-claims completely in the realm of faith, such is to ignore their possible objective theistic and historical nature (I,C; II,C):

    a. If it is claimed that miraculous events have occurred in history, as in the case of New Testament miracle-claims, then at least the objective, historical side of such a claim can be investigated. In other words, if it actually happened, a miracle can be examined, at least in some instances.

b. In the New Testament, the resurrection of Jesus is not only the central tenet of Christianity, but it is asserted that if Jesus did not rise from the dead, then faith is actually in vain (1 Cor. 15:1-20, especially vv. 14 and 17). Paul even supports his point that Jesus was raised by citing eyewitness, historical testimony to this fact (vv. 5-8). Under these circumstances, one could hardly claim that objective, factual interests in the resurrection are foreign to the New Testament.[14]

c. This objection also commits errors that are associated with the "leap of faith." If carried to its logical conclusion, it provides no objective basis for faith, including any reason why faith should be exercised in any certain beliefs or even that faith should be exercised at all.

6. Alternative theories which have been proposed to account for Jesus' resurrection on naturalistic grounds have failed to account for the known historical facts (II,C; V,D).

7. Several historians have supported the need to fully investigate miracle-claims and the resurrection of Jesus in particular (I,D; II,C).

D. Conclusion

We will not belabor the chief conclusion in this chapter, namely, that attempts to debunk the historicity of Jesus in whole or in part have failed for numerous reasons, such as those outlined above and in Chapters II-III. Usually such attempts ignore myriads of evidence that disprove these alternate hypotheses. Perhaps this is why most well-known, critical scholars also shun such theses.

The evidence pointed out in this chapter does reveal the negative conclusion concerning the failure of these misconceptions about Christianity. It also establishes some of the positive evidence in favor of the trustworthiness of Scripture, the historicity of Jesus and the nature of miracle-claims. Such evidence is quite formidable.

Notes

[1]See Hunter, *Bible and Gospel*, pp. 32-37.

[2]One example is found in the numerous claims in the New Testament that reveal that eyewitness information, evidence and factual and correct reporting are

all important priorities. See Luke 1:1-4; John 1:14; Acts 2:22-38; 17:30-31; 1 Cor. 15:1-20; Heb. 2:3-4; 2 Pet. 1:16-18; 1 John 1:1-3.

[3]See Sherwin-White, *Roman Society and Law*, pp. 186-193; Grant, *Jesus*, pp. 179-184, 199-201.

[4]Strauss, *Life of Jesus*, vol. I, pp. 408-412.

[5]For examples, see Mark 2:10-11; 10:45; 13:32; 14:36; 14:61-63; Matt. 11:27. Cf. John 8:58; 10:30; 14:6-11.

[6]Mark 2:1-12; Matt. 5:20-48; Isa. 9:6, 7; 53; Dan. 9:24-27.

[7]See Rom. 1:3-4; 9:5; 10:9-10; Phil. 2:6-11; Col. 1:19; 2:9; Titus 2:13.

[8]Cf. Matt. 5:18; Luke 16:16-17; Rom. 10:4, 9-11; Col. 2:16-17.

[9]Cf. Mark 1:14-15; Matt. 18:3-6; 25:31-46; Luke 18:28-30; 24:45-48; John 1:10-13; 6:47; 20:30-31.

[10]Cf. Rom. 6:23; 10:9-10; 1 Cor. 15:1-4.

[11]Acts 9:15-16; 22:21; Rom. 11:13-14.

[12]Matt. 28:19-20; Luke 24:47; John 10:16; Acts 1:8.

[13]See Gen. 12:3; Isa. 19:18-25, for examples.

[14]Again, even Bultmann asserts that Paul was attempting to produce objective evidence for the resurrection in this passage, although Bultmann himself disapproves. See his *Theology of the New Testament*, vol. 1, pp. 82, 295.

Appendix Two:
A Selected Scholarly Bibliography for
Chapter IV: Non-Christian Sources

(Each source, including primary documents, is listed in alphabetical order.)

A. Tacitus

Barnes, Timothy D. "Legislation Against the Christians." *Journal of Roman Studies* 58 (1968), 32-50.

Boissier, Gaston, *Tacite*. Paris: Hachette, etc., 1903.

Hadas, Moses. Editor. *The Complete Works of Tacitus*. Transl. by Alfred J. Church and William J. Brodribb. New York: Random House, 1942.

Mendell, Clarence W. *Tacitus, The Man and His Work*. New Haven: Yale University Press, 1957.

Sherwin-White, A. N. "The Early Persecutions and Roman Law Again." *Journal of Theological Studies* 3 (1952), 199-213.

de Ste. Croix, G. E. M. "The Persecutions: Christianity's Encounter with the Roman Imperial Government." *The Crucible of Christianity*. Ed. by Arnold Toynbee. New York: World Publishing Company, 1969.

Syme, Sir Ronald. *Tacitus*. 2 vols. Oxford: Clarendon Press, 1958.

B. Suetonius

Janne, H. "Impulsore Chresto." *Mélanges Bidez: Annuaire de l'Institute de Philologie et d'Histoire Orientales*. II (1934), 531-553.

Ramsay, Sir William. *The Church in the Roman Empire*. New York: G. P Putnam's Sons, 1893.

Safrai, S. and M. Stern. Editors. *The Jewish People of the First Century*. Vol. 1. Philadelphia: Fortress Press, 1974.

Scramuzza, Vincent. *The Emperor Claudius*. Harvard Historical Studies, 44. Cambridge: Harvard University Press, 1974.

Suetonius, Gaius. *The Twelve Caesars*. Transl. by Robert Graves. Baltimore: Penguin Books, 1957.

Wiefel, W. "The Jewish Community in Ancient Rome and the Origins of Roman Christianity." *The Romans Debate*. Ed. by K. P. Dornfried. Minneapolis: Augsburg Publishing House, 1977.

C. Josephus

Bentwich, Norman. *Josephus*. Philadelphia: The Jewish Publication Society of America, 1914.

Bienert, Walther. *Der alteste nichtchristliche Jesusbericht: Josephus über Jesus*. Halle: Akademischer Verlag, 1936.

Bruce, F. F. *Jesus and Christian Origins Outside the New Testament*. Grand Rapids: William B. Eerdmans Publishing Company. 1974.

Goldstein, Morris. *Jesus in the Jewish Tradition*. New York: Macmillan Press, 1950.

Josephus, Flavius, *The Works of Flavius Josephus*. Transl. by William Whiston. Grand Rapids: Kregel, 1974.

Klausner, Joseph. *Jesus of Nazareth*. London: Collier-Macmillan Press, 1929.

Laqueur, Richard. *Der jüdische Historiker Flavius Josephus*. Damstadt: Wissenschaftliche Buchgesellschaft, 1970.

Montifiore, H. W. *Josephus and the New Testament*. London: Mowbrays, 1962.

von Schlatter, Adolf. *Die Theologie des Judentums nach dem Bericht des Josephus*. Gutersloh: C. Bertelsmann, 1932.

Shutt, R. J. H. *Studies in Josephus*. London: SPCK, 1961.

Williamson, Geoffrey A. *The World of Josephus*. Boston: Little, Brown and Company, 1964.

D. Thallus

Bruce, F. F. *The New Testament Documents: Are They Reliable?* Grand Rapids: William B. Eerdmans Publishing Company, 1960.

Quasten, Johannes. *Patrology*. 3 vols. Utrecht-Antwerp: Spectrum Publishers, 1953, II: 137-138.

E. Pliny the Younger and Emperor Trajan

Pliny the Younger. *Pliny: Letters*. Transl. by William Melmoth. 2 vols. Cambridge: Harvard University Press, 1935.

Sherwin-White, A. N. *The Letters of Pliny: A Historical and Social Commentary*. Oxford: Clarendon Press, 1966.

Sherwin-White, A. N. "Why Were the Early Christians Persecuted? An Amendment." *Past and Present* 27 (1964), 23-27.

Vindman, L. *Étude sur la correspondance de Pline le Jeune avec Trajan*. Praha: Rozpravy Cheskoslovenske´Akademie Ved, 70 (1960), 87-106.

F. Emperor Hadrian

Eusebius Pamphilus. *Ecclesiastical History*. Transl. by Christian F. Cruse. Grand Rapids: Baker Book House, 1955.

G. Talmud

Epstein, I. Translator. *The Babylonian Talmud*. London: The Soncino Press, 1935.

Goldstein, Morris. *Jesus in the Jewish Tradition*. New York: Macmillan Press, 1950.

Hereford, R. T. *Christianity in Talmud and Midrash*. London: Williams and Norgate, 1903.

Jocs, Jacob. *The Jewish People and Jesus Christ*. London: SPCK, 1954.

Pranaitus, Iustin B. *The Talmud Unmasked: The Secret Rabbinical Teachings Concerning Christians*. New York: E. N. Sanctuary, 1939.

Schechter, Soloman. *Studies in Judaism*. Philadelphia: The Jewish Publication Society of America, 1908, 1924.

Strack, Hermann L. *Einleitung in Talmud und Midrasch*. München: Beck, 1921.

Wright, Dudley. *The Talmud*. London: Williams and Norgate, 1932.

H. Toledoth Jesu

Klausner, Joseph. *Jesus of Nazareth*. London: Collier-Macmillan Press, 1929.

Maier, Paul L. *First Easter*. New York: Harper and Row, Publishers, 1973.

I. Lucian of Samosata

Aerts, F. *Pereginus Proteus, een Kynieker uit de Ze eeuw na Kristus*. Dissertation; Löwen, 1931-1932.

Bagnani, G. "Pereginus Proteus and the Christians." *Historia* 4 (1955), 107-112.

Betz, E. "Lukian von Samosata und das Christentum." *Novum Testamentum* 3 (1959), 226-237.

————. *Lukian von Samosata und das Neue Testament, religionsgeschichtliche und paränetische Parallelen*. Berlin: Akademie-Verlag, 1961, 124-130.

Bompaire, Jacques. *Lucien écrivain; imitation et création*. Paris: E. de Boccard, 1958.

Caster, Marcel. *Lucien et la pensée religieuse de son temps*. Paris: Sociéte d'edition "Les Belles lettres," 1937.

Labriolle, P. De. "Lucien et les Chrétiens." *Les Humanitées* 4 (1929), 148-153.

Lane, William L. "Unexpected Light on Hebrews 13:1-6 from a Second Century Source." *Perspectives in Religious Studies* 9 (1982), 267-274.

Lucian of Samosata. *The Works of Lucian of Samosata*. Transl. by H.W. Fowler and F. G. Fowler. 4 vols. Oxford: Clarendon Press, 1905.

Schwartz, Jacques. *Biographie de Lucien de Samosate*. Bruxelles: Latomus, 1965.

Zeller, E. "Alexander und Peregrinus, ein Betrüger und ein Schwärmer." *Vortrage und Abhandlungen* 2 (1877), 154-188.

J. Mara Bar-Serapion

Bruce, F. F. *Jesus and Christian Origins Outside the New Testament*. Grand Rapids: William B. Eerdmans Publishing Company, 1974.

K. Gnostic Sources (in general)

Baur, Walter. *Orthodoxy and Heresy in Earliest Christianity*. Ed. by Robert Kraft and Gerhard Krodel. Philadelphia: Fortress Press, 1971.

Evans, Craig. "Jesus and Gnostic Literature." *Biblica* 62 (1981), 406-412.

Grant, Robert M. *Gnosticism and Early Christianity*. Revised edition. New York: Harper and Row, Publishers, 1966.

Jonas, Hans. *The Gnostic Religion*. Boston: Beacon Press, 1963.

Robinson, James M. Editor. *The Nag Hammadi Library*. New York: Harper and Row, Publishers, 1981.

L. Gospel of Truth

Arai, S. *Die Christologie des Evangelium Veritatis*. Leiden: E. J. Brill, 1964.

Grobel, Kendrick. *The Gospel of Truth*. London: Black, 1960.

Malinine, Michel, H. C. Peuch, and G. Quispel, *Evangelium Veritatis*. Zürich: Rascher, 1956.

Ringgren, Helmer. "The Gospel of Truth and Valentinian Gnosticism." *Studia Theologica* 18 (1964), 51-65.

Schenke, H.M. *Die Herkunft des sogenannten Evangelium Veritatis*. Göttingen: Vandenhoeck and Ruprecht, 1959.

M. Gospel of Thomas

Gärtner, Bertil. *The Theology of the Gospel According to Thomas*. Transl. by Eric J. Sharpe. New York: Harper and Brothers, 1961.

Schrage, Wolfgang. *Das Verhältnis des Thomas-Evangeliums zur Synoptischen Tradition und zu den Koptischen Evangelienübersetzungen*. Berlin: A. Topelmann, 1964.

Turner, H. E. W. and Montefiore, H. *Thomas and the Evangelists*. London: SCM Press, 1962.

Wilson, Robert M. *Studies in the Gospel of Thomas*. London: Mowbray, 1960.

N. Acts of Pontius Pilate

Justin Martyr. *First Apology: Anti-Nicene Fathers*. Ed. by Alexander Roberts and James Donaldson. Grand Rapids: William B. Eerdmans Publishing Company, 1973.

Tertullian. *Apology: Anti-Nicene Fathers*. Ed. by Alexander Roberts and James Donaldson. Grand Rapids: William B. Eerdmans Publishing Company, 1973.